"*Stealing Fire from the Gods* is like a rediscovered, ancient remedy for the ailing creative soul. Jim has tapped into a wellspring of lost knowledge that goes to the very core of the creative unconscious, unlocking the natural storyteller that is encoded in each and every one of us."
Bob Camp, Artist, Writer, Director, and Co-creator of
The Ren and Stimpy Show

"Anyone who is interested in structuring feeling and thoughts into words and story will find *Stealing Fire* stimulating and worthwhile. A lifetime labor of love, it provides the reader with insight, and an overview of the creative process through the history of story. I recommend it and congratulate Mr. Bonnet on his accomplishment."
Elliott Gould, Actor, Academy Award nominee

"Challenging and provocative. Bonnet is a thoughtful and highly intelligent writer whose lifetime of experience and insights have led him to an intriguing theory about how great stories are written. The Golden Paradigm is guaranteed to stimulate lively new debate on the age-old question."
David W. Rintels, Writer, Producer, winner of three Emmys, three Writers Guild Awards and two Peabody Awards

STEALING FIRE FROM THE GODS

Stealing Fire From
The Gods

A Dynamic New Story Model
for Writers and Filmmakers

James Bonnet

Published by Michael Wiese Productions, 11288 Ventura Blvd., Suite 821, Studio City, CA 91604, (818) 379-8799 Fax (818) 986-3408.

E-mail: wiese@earthlink.net

http://www.mwp.com

Cover design by The Art Hotel

Printed and Manufactured in the United States of America

Library of Congress Cataloging-in-Publication Data

Bonnet, James, 1938-
    Stealing fire from the gods : a dynamic new story model for writers and filmmakers / by James Bonnet.
             p.   cm.
    Includes bibliographical references and index.
    ISBN 0-941188-65-5
    1. Motion picture authorship.   2. Narration (Rhetoric)   I. Title.
PN1996.B66 1999   99-23166
    808.2'3 -- dc21   CIP

To my wife, Diane.
Without her love and support there would be
no book and I would have no life.

To my lifelong friend, Edward Cerny.
He introduced me to the books and ideas that
created the dream and the journey.

To my mentors,
Paton Price, Archer King, and Vincent J. Donehue,
for believing in me when I was little inclined
to believe in myself.

To my grandchildren,
Katie, Jimmy, Max, and Sam.
The love and joy we share
are little tastes of paradise.

*These are the mysteries that made fairy tales
and myths and all the great classics so powerful
and enduring—the secrets that made the
top-grossing films so successful—and the principles
that can guide you to a profound understanding
of story and the creative process and a true
mastery of the storymaker's art.*

TABLE OF CONTENTS

PREFACE

The knowledge contained in this book is a continuation of the work begun by Carl Jung, Joseph Campbell, Clarissa Pinkola Estes, and Erich Neumann, and will put forth revolutionary new ideas concerning the nature and purpose of story, the meaning of metaphor and myth, the creative unconscious, and the art of storymaking. It will introduce readers to an important new model of the human psyche called the Golden Paradigm, which was brought to light by intriguing new patterns discovered hidden in great stories. These new patterns reveal all of the psychic dimensions—their structure, their hierarchy, their conflicts, and their goals. These psychological models become story models when they are used to create new stories and will not only teach readers how to create contemporary stories that are significantly more successful and real than stories currently are, they will reveal important new details concerning how the conscious and creative unconscious minds can interact to form a creative partnership which is applicable not only to storymaking but to many different art forms, and can bring powerful inner resources to light.

Stealing Fire from the Gods will also introduce readers to a new phenomenon called the Storywheel, which brings all the different types of story together into one grand design. All great stories, ancient or modern, have a place on this wheel, and when looked at all together in this way, they reveal their deeper, more amazing secrets, not the least of which concern all of the life cycles we experience from birth to death. The archetypes, patterns of action, and cycles of transformation revealed in story are the same archetypes, patterns, and cycles which run through every individual and every group, and are being played out in all of life's important stages. If you understand these patterns, you can understand the world, your place in the scheme, and the paths which can lead you to higher states of consciousness and success.

A knowledge of story and the act of storymaking are essential links in a creative process that can reconnect us to our lost or forgotten inner selves. An understanding of story leads inevitably to an understanding of these dormant inner states and to a perception of the path which can lead us back to who we were really meant to be. In short, a vast, unrealized potential exists within us which a knowledge of story and storymaking can help to make real.

And because it contains important new knowledge about story that is not available anywhere else and is relevant no matter what kind of story, true or fiction, you want to create for whatever medium, this book will be of particular interest to writers and filmmakers, and those whose livelihood depends on an understanding of what makes a story great or successful. Its special emphasis is on how the great myths and legends were really created and how contemporary stories with that kind of magic and power can be created again. Armed with this new, deeper understanding of story, there is no limit to the power and art that can be created through them. Readers will know how to tap powerful creative sources deep within themselves and have the tools to use modern metaphors to create stories as significant for today as *King Arthur* and *The Iliad* were for their time.

Stealing Fire from the Gods will also be of special interest to the followers of the four authors mentioned above. Some important new discoveries have been made in their fields, most notably concerning the cracking of story's symbolic code and the new phenomena which this revealed. The secrets of great stories, it turns out, are the secrets of the human mind. And the study of story is the study of these remarkable phenomena. Every great story reveals some small piece of that magnificent mystery. Unlocking the secrets of story unlocks the secrets of the mind. Unlocking the secrets of the mind awakens the power of story within you. Work with that power and you can steal fire from the gods. Master that power and you can create stories that will live forever.

FOREWORD

When I first came to Hollywood thirty years ago as a young writer, I wanted to do something really significant with my talent. I wanted to create novels and films that had the quality of works by authors like Dostoyevsky and Tolstoy. So after working as a writer in television for several years, I decided I was ready to put everything else aside and write my first novel. I figured it would take about six months.

Two years later, after working eight hours a day, seven days a weeks, I found myself on page 600 with no end in sight. And I had the uncomfortable feeling that despite an already acknowledged skill I possessed concerning character, structure, and suspense, it wasn't going to work. Eventually, I had to admit there was much more to creating a great story than I thought. And the problem lay with the understanding of story itself. What was a story, really? And why hadn't I asked myself that question before?

I began talking to some of the important writers in town about story and was surprised to discover that no one seemed to know what a story really was. It was just something that was taken for granted. It was a knack. Part of your gift. You either had it or you didn't.

I asked Danny Arnold, who was an important writer-producer in television, what a story was, and he said, "You know, there are only seven basic plots: 'boy meets girl, boy loses girl,' and so on. That sounded promising, so I asked him what the other six were. He gave me a rather strange look and said, "I don't know."

Finally convinced that the answers to the questions I was asking about story weren't out there, I began to study stories and films in earnest on my own and to monitor what works.

The first thing I realized was that everything that "worked," worked because of an emotional response that was triggered in the audience. Story communicated by feelings. And the accumulation of those emotional responses was the basis of both entertainment and meaning.

The second thing I discovered was that structure had power. You could intensify the emotional response by how you arranged the incidents. The more dynamic the arrangement, the more powerful the emotional effect.

"My God," I thought, "there's something very important going on here. A story really is a kind of magic." I got very excited. I rushed back into the house from the office I built in the garage and told my wife what I had discovered. She seemed to share my enthusiasm, and in a moment of great inspiration, I raised my fist and declared, "I'm going to figure out what a story really is, if it takes me twenty years."

Twenty years later, after countless hours of hard work, when things had finally begun to jell, I reminded my wife of that conversation. She looked at me and said, "I wish you had said ten."

To this day, whenever I run into Julie Epstein, who wrote *Casablanca* and a number of other great films, he always asks me the same question: "How is your long-suffering wife?" And that mainly has to do with this very long and uncertain period of our lives.

Storymaking is the most important and misunderstood art form in the world today. Important because there is a desperate need for real stories which isn't being met, and misunderstood because no one seems to know what to do about it.

The knowledge of what stories actually are, how and why they evolved, the purpose they serve, and the mechanics of their creation has been largely misunderstood. And, if it was ever known, that knowledge, like the meaning of dreams, was lost and is just now being rediscovered.

The importance of story and the role it was meant to play in our lives is far greater than anyone has realized.

The goal of Astoria Filmwrights, the research project founded by the author, is to help rediscover and reveal this lost knowledge. The purpose of this book is to show the general reader and the professional storymaker how they can use this knowledge of story to dramatically transform their own and other people's lives.

Among the stories analyzed in this book you will find many of the most important myths, legends, and fairy tales (*The Iliad, The Odyssey, King Arthur, Amor and Psyche, Prometheus, Rumpelstiltskin, Jack and the Beanstalk,* etc.). You will also find several of the most important plays and literary classics (*Othello, Hamlet, Death of a Salesman, Macbeth, A Christmas Carol, The Count of Monte Cristo,* and *A Thousand and One Nights*); many of the most important classic and critically acclaimed films (*The Grapes of Wrath, Casablanca, On the Waterfront, Schindler's List, The Silence of the Lambs, All the President's Men, The Verdict, Braveheart, The Wizard of Oz, Snow White, Dracula, Ordinary People,* and *Shakespeare In Love*); and most of the all-time box-office hits (*E.T., Star Wars, Titanic, Pretty Woman, The Godfather, Armageddon, Superman, Jurassic Park, Indiana Jones, Mulan, Toy Story, Back to the Future, The Fugitive, Ghost,* and *Jaws*).

The one thing all of these old great stories, modern masterpieces, and all-time megahits have in common is the Golden Paradigm, the story model that was created from the secrets hidden in their flesh and bones.

PART ONE

THE NATURE AND PURPOSE OF STORY

INTRODUCTION

A long time ago, in far-off India, there was a merchant who lived in one of the northern provinces. He was very successful, but he was living in a dog-eat-dog world, not unlike our own, and was very unhappy.

"My God," he thought, "there has to be more to life than this."

So one day he went into the mountains to consult a famous guru who lived in one of the remote caves. And he asked the guru, "What is our true destiny?"

The guru was impressed by his sincerity and said, "I'm going to show you." He handed the merchant two potatoes and added, "But you have to do exactly what I say."

The merchant was eager to proceed, and the guru gave him his instructions.

"Take these two potatoes to the little stream at the bottom of the hill outside this cave. Very carefully wash both potatoes and eat them. Then return to the cave."

The merchant took the two potatoes and went down the hill to the stream. He very carefully washed the first potato and ate it. But while he was washing the second potato, an old woman came out of the forest at that spot and approached him. She was obviously very poor. She told him a sad story and begged him for something to eat. He was deeply moved. He gave her the second potato and she ate it.

The merchant felt rather good about what he had done and hurried back up the hill to the cave to report the incident to the guru. But much to his surprise when he told the guru what had happened, the guru was very upset.

"I told you to eat both potatoes," he admonished harshly.

The poor merchant was astonished. "I know, but—"

3

"No buts," the guru interrupted. "You were supposed to do exactly as I said." And he got so angry that he ordered the merchant out of his sight.

Extremely despondent, the merchant went down the mountain and returned to his village.

Two years passed, and near the end of that time the merchant started a new business, which turned out to be much more successful than the first. In fact, he became one of the richest men in all India. Two more years passed and he met the most beautiful woman he had ever seen in his life. They fell in love and were married. They had seven beautiful and healthy children, and everything these remarkable children did was a source of great pleasure and pride to their parents.

The merchant was held in such high esteem that he was elected governor of the entire province and people came from all around to seek his advice. He lived to be 120 years old and considered himself a very fortunate and happy man indeed.

And that was just the first potato.

*   *   *

This book is about those two potatoes. Story is about those two potatoes. Story is the wisdom that can guide you to your true destiny. All of the great myths, legends, and fairy tales have that power. If you understand their secrets, they can guide you to a full realization of your self.

Where did they get that extraordinary magic and power? How were they created? Can stories with that kind of magic and power ever be created again? We will answer all of these important questions in the first part of this book.

Great stories are created by powerful and mysterious inner processes. They are designed to guide us to our full potential and are as necessary to our well-being as fresh air. Understanding great stories means understanding these inner processes. And understanding these inner processes can lead to a profound understanding of our selves and the world.

CHAPTER 1

HOW THIS KNOWLEDGE
WAS DEVELOPED

The whole truth about story is like a large circle with a hundred dimensions. Each of these dimensions is so powerful that many of them can be isolated and made into a successful story or story film even if all of the other major dimensions are more or less unrealized. **Character** is one of these dimensions. **Action, structure (plot), imitations of life, metaphor, suspense, horror, and ironic comedy** are others. But there are many more. And a number of important filmmakers and novelists have created major successes by excelling in or perfecting just one or sometimes two of these powerful dimensions.

Eddie Murphy's use of character in *Beverly Hills Cop* is a good example. Like Charlie Chaplin and Woody Allen before him, Eddie Murphy is a man who understands the character he plays, and Axel Foley, the character he created in this film, is brilliantly conceived, containing many of the delightful attitudes and qualities we saw Murphy developing on *Saturday Night Live*. But the picture falls short in just about every other important dimension. The action is contrived, the plot and imitations of real life are extremely weak, metaphor is practically nonexistent, real suspense is lacking, and so on. But still the movie was a major box-office success—a testimony to the power of that one dimension, character.

A similar case can be made concerning Alfred Hitchcock's use of suspense, Stephen King's use of horror, Jim Abrahams's use of ironic comedy, Emile Zola's use of imitations of life, Sylvester Stallone's use of action in *Rambo: First Blood*, George Lucas's use of structure and special effects in *Star Wars*, and Steven Spielberg's use of metaphor and special effects in *Close Encounters of the Third Kind*. In all of these cases you will find one or two dominant dimensions brilliantly executed while many of the other important dimensions are more or less unrealized, and still they all enjoyed a phenomenal success.

Now, I am not putting down these storymakers because their work lacked the other dimensions, I am just trying to make clear how incredibly powerful the individual story dimensions are.

In *Star Wars*, for instance, the structure George Lucas used—which was, by his own admission, modeled after the formula outlined in Joseph Campbell's book *The Hero with a Thousand Faces*—is so powerful and universal, that despite a number of other weaknesses, the film remains one of the most successful ever made.

Similarly, in *Close Encounters* Steven Spielberg's use of the metaphor of benign forces coming from outer space made such a profound psychological impact that it set the stage for Spielberg to become the most successful filmmaker of all time.

So these individual dimensions are powerful indeed.

The problem is that each time someone discovers one of these important dimensions, the affects are so tremendous that they tend to think they have discovered the whole truth about story and not just a part. So their thinking becomes circumscribed and they end up specializing in that dimension—i.e., creating stories and films that revolve around character, action, adventure, suspense, comedy, or horror, and so on—rather than incorporating all of the dimensions in the stories they create.

The same thing is true on the theoretical side, where a hundred different schools of thought have sprung up based on the different dimensions that were discovered. This is true from Aristotle and John Dryden all the way to John Howard Lawson, Lajos Egri, and Joseph Campbell. Here again, because of the extraordinary affect of any one dimension, they tend to regard the part they have discovered as the whole thing. Their thinking becomes polarized. And rather than realizing that they each discovered something valuable, they end up attacking each other. The result is a large number of one-sided, incomplete, and faulty story models.

In contrast, my strategy has been to make my thinking as non-specialized and non-polarized as possible, and to bring together as much information from as many different fields as I could to create one grand, unified theory of story. I have tried to accomplish this by assuming that the whole truth about story was, in fact, like a large circle with at least a hundred dimensions, and that each of these other important ideas was one of the dimensions in that much larger circle. The models I created from this knowledge became my reference points. Then I would use these reference points to develop new information. Each time I learned something new, the current model would be adjusted and that would create a new reference point.

Then in March of 1989 something rather extraordinary happened: one of these elements tumbled into the center and the rest began to constellate around it. And when this transformation was complete, a new model, the Golden Paradigm, had emerged. Previous models, like those of Aristotle and Joseph Campbell, had been created by the observation of the things that all stories had in common. This new model was being created by their differences. And the new patterns revealed by these differences were not only the key to story, but the key to some important secrets about life as well.

CHAPTER 2

WHY THE OLD GREAT STORIES WERE CREATED

The element that tumbled into the center was "change"—the fact that our lives, like everything else in the universe, are in a process of continual evolution and change. Story has an important role to play in helping to guide and regulate that change.

According to story (which is to say, according to the hidden meanings being revealed by these new patterns), we all possess a vast, unrealized potential. There is a path to that potential, and a creative unconscious force that uses great stories (and also dreams) to guide us along that path. In a former time (perhaps as long ago as the cave paintings in Europe), communication between our conscious selves and this creative unconscious force was apparently excellent; we made these special passages easily, and everything was great. Then something happened. The world took a turn for the worse and communication between us and this creative unconscious force was cut off. We lost touch with our selves. We lost touch with the real meaning of story and dreams and we got stuck somewhere far from our full potential. Our lives became much less meaningful and far more difficult.

All of this is revealed in story. And part of what I intend to teach in this book, besides how to become a significant storymaker capable of creating great stories, is how to use this knowledge to mend these broken connections and recover that vast potential.

The Vast Potential

To recount our evolutionary path, we evolved from reptiles to mammals to primates to early man to Homo sapiens, man the wise. According to story, this evolutionary path proceeded in cycles, in a series of advances and declines. At the top of the upside of every cycle there was a psychological surge and a psychological paradise was achieved. This psychological paradise was not a lost civilization like Atlantis, but a brief moment in history when all of the talents and powers that had been so painstakingly evolved up to that point were being fully realized. But also contained in this paradise were the seeds and flaws that would bring about another decline, an alienation from the higher spiritual, mental, and emotional dimensions that had been achieved. The old paradise had to be shut down, taken apart, and rebuilt in order to advance to a new higher one.

I will describe the mechanisms revealed in story which bring about these declines when we talk about the dynamics of the passage, but I will outline one example here.

Commensurate with having achieved the last major advance was a knowledge of agriculture. The application of this knowledge led to an abundance of food and a sedentary life, which led to overpopulation, which led to a fierce competition for resources, which led to warring states—a downside condition from which we are yet to recover. The pressures of that decline helped transform us from fully awakened and enlightened spiritual beings into egocentric, patriarchal warriors with little need for higher powers. Or so we thought.

Today we find ourselves at the tail end of the latest downside cycle in an age which the Hindus call Kali Yuga, the age of alienation and discord. This is the society we have to conform to, so this is where we get stuck. What we could gain if we chose to recapture the rest of this evolutionary cycle is the **vast potential**. It is our unrealized mental, emotional, physical, and spiritual genius, our hidden talents, our higher consciousness, a profound capacity to love, our extraordinary but latent intuitive, creative, and healing powers. Our charisma. Our power to influence the world, transcend duality, experience ultimate truth, and so on. It is who we were really meant to be. It is what the Indian merchant would have achieved if he had eaten the second potato. Psychologists and scientists are fond of saying that we use only ten percent of our brain's capacity. The vast potential is the

10

other, unrealized, unachieved ninety percent. We get little tastes and inklings of it throughout our lives, little tingling sensations that creep up our spines and tell us there's something more to life than we're experiencing. Much more.

The Path

The path is the journey of our lives, the cycles of change and growth that are necessary to reach this vast potential. These emotional, psychological, and spiritual passages correspond roughly to our physical growth cycles from birth to death. They last from three to five years and involve us in certain essential activities. As children, we have to experience certain things if we are to mature properly. Then, as we get older, we have to be educated, establish our careers, find suitable mates, raise a family, serve our community, serve our country, serve our God, and so on.

If we fail to make these passages successfully, which most of us do, there are serious consequences. We get stuck. We stop growing. We feel lost and unfulfilled. But if we succeed, the rewards are tremendous.

The wisdom necessary to make these passages successfully is buried like a treasure deep in the unconscious. Great stories bring that wisdom to consciousness. The information contained in great stories is all about these passages and how to make them in such a way as to achieve these higher states of being.

Our Conscious Self

By our conscious self, I mean all of the things we are consciously aware of—our thoughts, feelings, mental images, and so on. The ego is the center of consciousness, and it performs the conscious functions—rational thinking, creative thinking, decision making, and so on. The ego is that which we usually refer to when we say "I." And it is the conscious part of us that needs to be guided and directed by story along the path.

Our Unconscious Self

The **unconscious self** is the creative unconscious force that would guide us, if we weren't cut off. It goes by a lot of different names.

Carl Jung called it the self or the collective unconscious. Freud called it the superego, the libido, and the id. Erich Neumann called it the creative unconscious. Buddhists call it Buddha Consciousness. Religions call it God, the Holy Spirit, the Devil, or the soul. George Lucas called the positive aspect the Force. Obi-Wan Kenobi (Alec Guinness) in *Star Wars*, an agent of the Force, is without a doubt a metaphor for this guiding self.

I usually call it the **creative unconscious**. The unconscious has a positive and a negative side, but when they are both working together to build consciousness, the negative unconscious becomes a reluctant ally and the creative unconscious is formed. I like that concept, so I like that term. I also like the **hidden truth** or the **self**.

According to Carl Jung, the hidden truth is the ancient wisdom that has been accumulating in our psyches since the beginning of evolution. And that is basically what I mean when I talk about our evolutionary path and unrealized potential—that a record of this evolutionary path has been kept and stored deep in the unconscious like a treasure. It is probably stored somewhere in the DNA. It may be a manifestation of the DNA itself.

Whatever it is, or whatever you call it, doesn't matter. It is the creative unconscious source of all of the higher universal intelligence, wisdom, and truth we possess. And one of its main functions is to guide us along the path that will transform this vast unconscious potential energy into a useful conscious energy—in short, to a full realization of our selves. This process expands, strengthens, and elevates consciousness. It is what so-called "higher" consciousness is about, and when creative people say they have tapped into the source, this is what they mean. This is the source.

Great stories and dreams, as I said, are two important ways the creative unconscious self communicates its hidden knowledge to consciousness.

But why great stories and dreams?

Great stories and dreams are visual **metaphors**. They are symbolic languages. And the creative unconscious self uses these visual metaphors to express its hidden wisdom to consciousness.

The creative unconscious and its hidden treasure exist in the brain as energy. To be experienced consciously, this raw energy has to be translated into a form the conscious mind can assimilate and understand. The forms of choice that the creative unconscious uses are feelings (which we'll examine when we talk about the creative process) and the visual languages of fantasy, story, and dream.

There's nothing mysterious about this process. The brain is doing this all the time. It's a basic brain function. It's the way we see, for instance. When we look at an object like a person or a tree, photoelectric energy is reflected off that object, enters the eye, travels along the optic nerve, and is translated back into a visual image somewhere in the brain. The creative unconscious simply utilizes this image-making mechanism to express itself to consciousness.

"Myths and dreams," according to Joseph Campbell, "are manifestations in image form [metaphors] of all of the energies of the body, moved by the organs, in conflict with each other."

In the 1984 movie *Starman,* forgotten by most, but worth viewing for one particular reason, you can see an excellent metaphor for this process. At the beginning of the film a bright ball of alien energy reaches the Earth from outer space, enters a house, and using a photograph from a family album, transforms itself into the dead husband of the lonely widow who lives in the house. This is a perfect metaphor for what I'm describing. The widow, like our conscious selves, could not relate to the alien in its

13

energy form. So the alien, like the unconscious energy, translates itself into a form the widow can relate to and deal with—an image of her dead husband. The creative unconscious does exactly this when it translates its energy into a fictional visual form made up of everyday things we can consciously relate to and interpret.

I'll give you two simple examples. The first is a dream.

A year or two after Diane and I settled in Los Angeles, we were living in a small house in Studio City. I haunted the used-book stores in the neighborhood and one day discovered a book by Jay Hambridge called *Dynamic Symmetry*. The premise of the book was that the extraordinary beauty achieved by the early Greeks in their art and architecture was due to a golden proportion, which was based on a natural progression of numbers. This progression of numbers was found in nature and governed the distribution of leaves, the arrangement of seeds in a sunflower, and the proportions of the human body. Called the Fibonacci series after the man who first described it, the progression begins with the number 1, and each succeeding number in the series is formed by the addition of the two previous numbers—that is, 1, 1, 2, 3, 5, 8, 13, 21, 34, 55, 89, and so on. I could find these special number ratios in the distribution of leaves and in the sunflower (34 counterclockwise spirals, overlaid by 55 clockwise spirals, overlaid by 89 counterclockwise spirals), but for the life of me I couldn't fathom where they were in the human body. It obsessed me like a riddle I couldn't solve. I fell asleep one night pondering this puzzle and had this dream. A muscular right arm reached into the darkness of the dreamscape and, slowly bending at each joint, formed this pattern and revealed that it was the bone lengths of the arm, hand, and finger digits that contained this golden proportion. Needless to say, I was astounded that the unconscious mind had this ability to give me such a direct answer.

The second example is a story—*Jack and the Beanstalk.*

I've known about this story since my mother began telling it to me when I was four or five years old. But I was well into my forties before I realized that the hidden truth being communicated by this remarkable tale had to do with how these lost or unrealized potentials can be recovered.

THE TALE

Jack lives with his mother in a remote valley and they are very poor. So poor, in fact, they have to sell the very thing they're living off—the family cow. And Jack's mother entrusts her young son with that very important task.

On the way to town, the boy meets a man who offers to trade some magic beans for the cow. Jack is excited by the prospect of owning magic beans, so the deal is made, and he rushes home to tell his mother.

"Ma, Ma, look what I got for the cow!" And he holds out his hand to show her the magic beans.

Not surprisingly, the poor woman is very upset. Any fool can see they're just ordinary beans. She grabs the beans, throws them out the window, sends the boy to bed without any dinner, and has a good cry.

In the morning when Jack wakes up, he discovers a remarkable thing. An enormous beanstalk has appeared during the night and grown all the way up to the sky. Jack climbs to the top of the beanstalk and discovers a gigantic house sitting on top of the clouds. He knocks on the door and it is opened by the giant's wife. He relates what happened and asks for something to eat.

The giant's wife is sympathetic and offers to feed him, but on the way to the kitchen she warns him to be careful because her husband, the giant, likes to eat little boys like him for breakfast. And sure enough, as Jack is sitting at the kitchen table eating some porridge, he hears the approaching giant exclaim, "Fee Fie Fo Fum–I smell the blood of an Englishman!"

Jack panics and hides in the cupboard, just narrowly escaping detection and perhaps even death.

The giant enters the kitchen. He looks around, sees nothing suspicious and relaxes. Then he takes several large sacks of gold from his hiding place of treasures, sits at the kitchen table to count his gold, and eventually falls asleep. Jack sees his chance, sneaks out of the cupboard, grabs the sacks of gold, and makes his escape down the beanstalk.

Jack and his mother share the gold with the other poor people in the valley, and for awhile everything is all right, but eventually the money runs out. So Jack makes a couple of more trips up the beanstalk and gets two of the giant's other treasures: the goose that lays the golden eggs and the magic harp. The last time, the giant wakes up and almost catches him. There's a desperate chase, but Jack gets to the bottom of the beanstalk first. He chops it down and the giant falls to his death.

And so ends *Jack and the Beanstalk*, the encoded message from the creative unconscious self.

The treasures—the bags of gold, the goose that lays the golden eggs, the magic harp—are the metaphors, the "manifestations in image form," representing some of the lost potential I've been talking about, and the story is a simple blueprint showing us how this lost potential (these lost inner psychic treasures) can be recovered by the skillful use of the creative imagination. It begins with a creative inspiration; that's what the magic beans represent. Jack is inspired by the idea of possessing magic. This creative inspiration leads to a nonconformist, impractical act: he sells the practical cow. The impractical act leads to consequences: the heat he gets from his mother. These consequences lead to isolation: he is sent to his room without any dinner. The isolation and hunger lead to the awakening of the creative imagination: the beanstalk. The creative imagination, which can bridge the gap between the conscious and unconscious worlds, puts him in touch with his creative unconscious self and the chance to recover some of that lost, unrealized potential, but it involves taking certain risks, and he has to confront, outwit, and destroy a big ugly giant to do it. The big ugly giant represents the negative energies which keep the potential treasures captive and prevent their easy recovery.

If you are an artist and you follow a real creative inspiration to its fulfillment, you will discover this trail. The creative inspiration will make you aware of other worlds hidden in your soul, and you will realize that if you are to be truly happy, there are other important things that have to be accomplished in life besides just making money. This will lead you to impractical acts. You will want to quit law school and go to Paris to study art, New York to study music, or Hollywood to break into film. These impractical acts will lead to consequences: the disapproval you are going to get from your parents, your spouse, or other well-meaning, interested parties. Whenever you try to step away from the mainstream, there will be conflict and resistance. These consequences can lead to alienation and isolation, and you may find yourself alone in a garret in Greenwich Village or San Francisco with nothing to eat. Alone and hungry, you may find that your creative imagination will bridge the gap between the conscious and creative unconscious worlds (isolation, meditation, and fasting are well-known avenues to the creative unconscious). Then if you have the courage to pursue these creative adventures, despite the difficulties, you can confront your ogres (negative energies) and one by one recover all of these lost treasures, until finally in the end all of these negative energies have been transformed and you have filled up the lost and missing parts of your self.

All of this is revealed in that simple story. It's a realistic look at what you will constantly face if you choose a life of art—the good news and the bad. And if you reread the story with that in mind, you will realize it was always there waiting for you to discover its secret meanings. It is a special mirror that lets you look into your own soul. And a story that can do that has real power and can live forever.

Great stories, then, are like collective dreams. They originate in the creative unconscious and have the same relation to society as a whole that the dream has to the individual. They both utilize the same archetypal symbols, but the meanings hidden in great stories are universal, whereas the meanings hidden in dreams are usually personal.

CHAPTER 3

How The Old Great Stories Were Created

Now, if the creative unconscious used these great stories to communicate with us, then it must have participated in their creation. And so it did. These old great stories, which really could change people's lives, were not authored by individuals the way stories are today but were evolved naturally and instinctively by unconscious processes in oral traditions. And even if they started out as made-up or true stories, revelations or dreams, they still ended up for long periods of time in oral traditions, and that became the principal dynamic behind their creation.

The process goes like this: It begins with a real or imagined incident or event that is worth repeating, something so intriguing that we're compelled to repeat it. It is passed along by word of mouth, from person to person and from generation to generation, until it's been told and retold millions of times and exists in a hundred different versions around the world.

Each time the story is retold it changes. This is due to certain natural but **curious tendencies of the mind**—the tendency, for instance, to **remember** things that make a strong impression and to **forget** things that don't impress us very strongly. There is also a tendency to **exaggerate** or **minimize**, to **glorify** or **ennoble**, to **idealize** or **vilify**. Beyond that, there's a natural, unconscious tendency to **analyze** things, to take them apart and put them back together in different combinations (**recombination**), and a natural tendency to **simplify** or **edit**. The tendency to conserve energy in nature is very strong in everything we do, including how we organize and store our thoughts and memories. These are all things we're very aware of.

We've all heard about the three-foot-long fish someone caught that was, in reality, barely eighteen inches, or seen someone make a minor problem seem like the end of the world, or perhaps we recall something that was truly horrendous as being no big deal. Or we become convinced that someone we knew back then was a genius, a world-class athlete, or the most beautiful girl in the world. I had a distant relative pass away who was, in reality, something of a bastard. But after his death, only the good things were being remembered and everyone began to believe he was one of the nicest guys that ever lived. Shakespeare reminds us that the opposite is also true. In *Julius Caesar* he tells us: "The evil that men do lives after them, the good is oft interred with their bones." Hitler would be an obvious example. If he ever did a decent thing in his life, you're never going to hear about it. He's been completely and justifiably vilified.

We experience these curious tendencies constantly. They are a significant part of our everyday lives. We all know how hard it is to get a story straight or accurately remember something we've been told, or even experienced, if it hasn't been written down. You tell someone close to you something exciting that happened (an incident worth repeating) and when you hear it repeated later that week or even later that day, it's been severely changed. It's the cause of many serious misunderstandings. Well, you can imagine what happens to a story that has spent hundreds of years in an oral tradition. It has been thoroughly and completely changed.

There have been numerous experiments documenting this phenomenon. I saw one not long ago on PBS on one of their science programs. In this particular experiment, twenty children were lined up on stage. A story was whispered into the ear of the first child and she was told to repeat it. She whispered it to the boy next to her and he whispered it into the ear of the girl next to him, and so on. Then everyone laughs when they hear the last child's version because of the way it's been completely changed.

The important thing to remember here is that these are unconscious, instinctual processes. These old great stories were being created by the creative unconscious mind. The creative unconscious seized the incident worth repeating, and slowly over time, using these curious tendencies, helped sculpt it into a marvelous story that contained powerful bits of that hidden truth. No one had to do anything consciously but repeat the story. And even if there was conscious involvement (i.e., the desire to use the story to instruct or entertain or even to change it), those desires and changes were prompted by feelings which originated in the unconscious, so the end result would be the same.

Examples from History

We can see how this works if we look at certain important historical figures and examine how the real incidents which surrounded their lives and were worth repeating were evolved by oral traditions into marvelous and even miraculous tales that contained important bits of this hidden truth I've been speaking of.

The first involves Achilles and the Trojan wars. While there is no historical record of these events, most scholars, and most people for that matter, believe there really was a place called Troy and a Trojan war which took place on the western shores of Turkey sometime around 1200 B.C. Many important archaeologists, Heinrich Schliemann among them, have devoted their lives to discovering the sites of these ancient events.

The real Trojan war, then, was the incident worth repeating, and Achilles, the greatest warrior fighting on the Greek side, was the Audie Murphy of his day (Audie Murphy being the most decorated soldier in World War II). It is controversial whether someone named Homer, the accredited author of *The Iliad* and *The Odyssey,* the famous legendary accounts of these wars, actually existed, but assuming he did, the true story of the Trojan war had already spent four hundred years in the oral tradition before he put his poetic stamp on it, and another three or four hundred years in the oral tradition after his contribution, before it was actually written down. In that time it had evolved from the real incidents worth repeating into a truly miraculous tale in which the swift-footed Achilles has become the nearly immortal and invincible son of Theta, a sea goddess—all of the other gods, including Zeus, have taken sides and are playing active roles in the war, and all manner of miraculous things are occurring. These immortal characters and miraculous occurrences have a psychological significance which goes far beyond anything a factual account of the real incidents could ever have conveyed. They do, in fact, reveal an excellent picture of the human psyche in transformation, and more specifically, the consequences of anger on that transformation—all things we would have difficulty finding in a real account of that war.

Alexander the Great is another good subject to study in this regard because there is both a good historical record in the West as well as a rich tradition of legends in the East. In the West there are no real legends because there was always the real historical record standing as a reference to contradict them. But in the fabulous East, in places like India and Persia, where there was no historical record, he entered the oral tradition and all manner of fanciful and legendary stories evolved—"Alexander Searches for the Fountain of Youth," "Alexander Explores the Bottom of the Sea," and so on. These legendary stories, shaped and molded by these unconscious processes, contain the hidden wisdom we spoke of which the history does not. The historical record reveals reality, the legends that evolved in and were sculpted by the oral traditions contain the hidden, inner truth. The Fountain of Youth, for instance, like the goose that lays golden eggs, is another "manifestation in image form" (metaphor) of the lost potential I've been talking about. And Alexander's legendary adventures, like Jack's, are treasure maps that can, if followed, lead to its recovery.

King Arthur is another interesting case. Many scholars believe that this legendary English king was evolved from a real general named Arturus. General Arturus lived in the fifth century A.D. and won ten consecutive battles against the Saxons before he was finally killed. If these scholars are correct, then after only five or six hundred years in the oral tradition this real general Arturus had been transformed into the legendary King Arthur who wielded a magic sword named Excalibur, consorted with a sorcerer named Merlin, founded Camelot, established the Round Table, and sent his chivalrous knights on a quest for the Holy Grail. And here again, like *The Iliad* and *Jack and the Beanstalk*, the legends surrounding King Arthur have a great deal to tell us about our inner selves, our vast potential, and our true destinies, while the brief historical record of General Arturus has probably had very little effect on any of our lives.

The curious tendencies of the mind that drive this natural story-making process, and which we tend to regard as shortcomings, turn out to be the **artistic tools of the imagination**. And the creative unconscious used these tools to create these great stories. This vital information was being programmed into them bit by bit with each of these changes. The tellers of stories were only having fun, but in fact, they were helping to create and then pass this information along. And this is where these old great stories get their power. These little bits of hidden truth have real power and charisma.

Myths are stories that have evolved to such an extent that the truth they contain has become so charismatic and obvious that religions are formed around them. All of the great religions have mythological stories as their justification and the source of their truth.

There are no better examples of this than Moses and Jesus. Again, no historical record, but most people believe, or are willing to concede, that a real historical Jesus and Moses did in fact exist. After six hundred years in the oral tradition, Moses was turning staffs into serpents and performed any number of other miracles for the edification of the Pharaoh including the parting of the Red Sea. And after only forty to eighty years in the oral tradition, Jesus had become the result of a virgin birth and had risen from the dead. There's no way to calculate what effect a factual record of the real events surrounding these important figures might be having on our lives, but it's safe to say there have been very few things in life that have had a greater effect on the world than the stories that evolved from those real events.

It is, in fact, the function of religion to utilize the truth revealed in these great stories to help guide their charges back to their original nature. Religion, when it is not corrupt, is a conscious, organized effort to get people to go back up this path and they get their marching orders from stories. Instead of calling it individuation (Jung's term for the full realization of the self) or reaching your full potential, they call it recovering your lost innocence or reunion with God.

It may also be worth noting here that when the real incidents that were worth repeating entered the oral tradition and evolved into myths and legends, they became not less true, but more true, because now they contained some powerful bits of the hidden truth. The real incidents as they evolve become less reflective of the outer circumstances and more reflective of the hidden, inner reality. I leave it to the individual to decide which they think is more important.

CHAPTER 4

WHY THE OLD GREAT STORY TAKES THE FORM THAT IT DOES

The purpose of great stories, then, is to guide us to our full potential. Now let's talk about the nature of story—why the old great story takes the form it does and why its secrets have to be concealed.

The ego that would be guided through these passages presents the self with some pretty thorny problems, the principal one being that it simply doesn't want to do it. We have an incredibly strong, built-in resistance to change. In most cases, we would much rather hold on to some pleasant (or even unpleasant) current situation than give up everything and venture into the unknown. Real life is a serious and deadly game. It involves taking significant risks and facing unpleasant realities and truths.

Someone once asked a buddha about these truths and the buddha showed him a bowl of worms and said, "If you would understand these truths, then you would have to eat this bowl of worms."

The man shuddered with disgust and walked away. The point of the story being, of course, that the truths we have to face in life are sometimes like eating a bowl of worms. They can be that unpleasant.

Two days after I was thinking of using that little story in the seminars I was preparing, I had this dream: I was riding in the back of a convertible. We were approaching a crossroads and there was something there I didn't want to see, so I covered my face with my hands and said, "No, no. I don't want to look." But then, to my credit, I peeked through my fingers, anyway, and this is what I saw.

There was a dinky little RV sitting at the crossroads. On the side of the RV, where the utilities are usually plugged in, there were four very organic-looking holes. And while I was watching, a dozen or so very fat six-foot worms came pouring out of these holes onto the ground.

I woke up in a cold sweat. And it took several hours before I realized what the dream meant. The journey I was about to begin (i.e., the taking of the knowledge of story I had discovered to market) wasn't going to be a pleasant one. I could see that in the dream because I don't like traveling in RVs, especially this type, which was really just a pickup truck with a small aluminum camper on it. And, furthermore, the worms I was going to have to swallow on this journey weren't itty-bitty little worms like in the buddha's bowl, they were big fat ones that were six feet long.

It's not the kind of thing you look forward to.

So we are reluctant to make these passages and we have to be lured or pushed into the process. The strategy that the creative unconscious uses to lure us is the same ingenious strategy nature always uses when it teaches. It covers its medicine with a **sugar coat**. It hides all of the secret wisdom and purpose of story in an irresistible package with a sugar coat. The sugar coat in story is, of course, the entertainment dimensions. And the recipient doesn't even know what's happening—like a mother secretly hiding vitamin pills in her child's Twinkie.

You can see this strategy very clearly in children's games, and for this reason they are very much like a great story. Games are fun to play and that's why children love to experience them, but they have an important and secret underlying purpose—to exercise the physical body, develop social skills, etc. In other words, they have an important purpose which the child is not aware of and a sugar coat. The sugar coat lures the children into the experience and they become better prepared for life while they're having fun. If you take the fun out of the game, the child loses interest. If you take the entertainment out of the story, the same thing happens. We lose interest.

Sex is another obvious example of nature's use of this strategy. We are lured into the experience by a seductive sugar coat (the promise of romance and pleasure), but the real, underlying purpose has to do with procreation and the continuation of the species.

Motherhood is another example. Women are lured into the experience by some very pleasant maternal instincts, then find out about morning sickness, labor pains, and teenagers later on, when it's too late to change their minds.

In all of these examples you will find a sugar coat (the promise of fun, fulfillment, or pleasure) luring the person into an experience that has an important but hidden underlying purpose. In short, when nature wants something to happen, it doesn't rely on our having good judgment or common sense. It uses the promise of fun and pleasure to get the job done without any hassle.

The movie *Fatal Attraction* can give you a hint of how this process might work in a modern film. We were lured into the theatre by the promise of a great entertainment—a safe terror. That was the word of mouth on this picture. "You've got to see this movie. It is *so* scary." That was the sugar coat. Then we came out of the theatre with some very unsettling feelings about having affairs, as if there was a hidden message warning us of danger.

CHAPTER 5

How The Great Story
Does Its Work

The purpose of story, then, is to guide us to our full potential, and the nature of story is to conceal that purpose in an enticing sugar coat that lures us into the experience. But if the purpose is concealed, then how does it do its work?

The great story does its work in several important ways:

First, it stimulates our imaginations by provoking personal **fantasies**, which lead to the desire for actions in the real world. Then it gives us a **taste**, by way of a special feeling, of what it might be like if we were actually to make one of these passages and accomplish some of these things.

When a young girl hears *Sleeping Beauty* for the first time, delicious feelings are awakened which that child has never felt before, and she begins to have fantasies about meeting a real Prince Charming of her own. And when the Prince kisses the Sleeping Beauty and she wakes up, the child feels a sensation which is like a taste of paradise—a taste of what it would feel like if this really happened to her. She wants that feeling again in real life. She longs for it and pursues it in life as a dream.

The same thing happens when we experience a story like *Lost Horizon*. Shangri-la, like paradise, Utopia, or any promised land, is another metaphor for the higher states of consciousness and bliss that can be realized. And when we encounter these images in a story, we get chills and other special feelings which can convince us that such lofty places or spiritual states of mind actually exist and can be achieved. We long to reexperience them and pursue them in life as a goal.

Carl Jung explains it this way: "The auditor experiences some of the sensations but is not transformed. Their imaginations are stimulated: they go home and through personal fantasies begin the process of transformation for themselves."

And all of this happens automatically. The story recipients need not be consciously aware that the story is intentionally trying to influence and guide them.

Having lured us into the adventure by **fantasies** and a **taste**, the great story then provides us with a **road map** or treasure map, which outlines all of the actions and tasks we have to accomplish in order to complete one of these passages, and a **tool kit** for solving all of the problems that have to be solved to accomplish the actions and tasks. Every great story will divulge a little more of this truth, and bit by bit each step of the passage is revealed. Again, all of this is going on without the story recipient's conscious knowledge that it's happening.

How does it do that? By **meaningful connections**.

If it's a great story, we will remember it, and over time, we will make meaningful associations and connections with our real-life situations.

A lawyer friend of mine was recently telling me about a difficult case he was involved in, and how he had suddenly realized why it was so difficult. He had been acting quixotically. He had been fighting windmills. Acting quixotically and fighting windmills, of course, come from Don Quixote. Without even being aware of it, my lawyer friend had made a meaningful connection with his real-life situation. And suddenly having that realization, he was able to resolve the difficulty. And he hadn't even been aware that it was happening, that the metaphor in Don Quixote was there waiting for him when he needed it.

Another friend came to me after seeing *Groundhog Day* and confessed, "This is my life. I'm constantly reliving the same day." A third friend confided he was like the beast in *Beauty and the Beast*. These are **meaningful connections**. And if you will take the trouble to study them, you will find they are also providing you with the solutions to these very common problems. These lessons learned, we can transform ourselves back into princes and real human beings.

The more hidden truth the story contains, the more appealing it will be, the more relevant it will be to our lives, and the more likely we are to remember it. We'll cherish and work with it all of our lives, then we'll pass it on to our children.

No one story, as I've said, contains the whole truth. The process is accumulative. Each story contributes a little bit of this vital information. We can be affected by many different stories at the same time. We relate them to our lives when and if we need them and make the necessary course corrections.

It was more than thirty years from the time I first heard *Rumpelstiltskin* until I realized that the secrets hidden in that marvelous tale were about the creative process and how the mind is organized.

In *Rumpelstiltskin* and many stories like it, some endangered princess has to perform some impossible task like transforming a pile of straw into gold by morning or she'll lose her head. Then some miraculous helper like Rumpelstiltskin comes to her rescue and accomplishes the task for her while she sleeps.

Being a writer, I would often fall asleep at night worrying about certain difficult story problems I hadn't been able to solve during that workday. And just as often a marvelous solution to those problems would pop into my head as I was waking up the following morning. Naturally, I wondered who or what was solving those problems.

Suddenly, one day I made the connection. "My God," I exclaimed. "It's Rumpelstiltskin!"

The miraculous little helper was a metaphor, a personification in image form of some unconscious problem-solving mechanism. The secret hidden in the marvelous story had something important to reveal about the creative process and how our minds function. Namely, that inside our minds there is an unconscious problem-solving mechanism (a Rumpelstiltskin) that continues to work and transform our serious problems (the straw) into precious insights (the gold), while our conscious minds are asleep. Another little piece of the puzzle had been revealed.

And, finally, the great story guides this whole process with incredible insights and **wisdom**.

In *A Christmas Carol*, when the Ghost of Christmas Future is showing Scrooge his own tombstone, the kneeling, pathetic, nearly repentant Scrooge asks him, "Are these things that will be or things that may be?" The answer to that question, and the point of the whole story, is that these are things that "will be" if he does nothing, and things that "may be" if he does something about it, if he repents and changes his character. If he changes his character, he will change his future. In other words, at any given moment we have a certain destiny. And if we're not content with that destiny, we can do something about it. We can transform our futures by transforming ourselves. If we change who we are, if we awaken our humanity, we can change our destiny. That's good news.

Believe it or not, there's something similar and equally profound in the movie *Back to the Future*. Having seen *Back to the Future, Part II*, and having no desire to see Part III, I have concluded the profundity in Part I got there by accident, but nevertheless, it's there.

At the beginning of the story, we meet Michael J. Fox and his family. His mother is an alcoholic and his rather pathetic father a serious wimp and a miserable failure. And they're living in a hovel of mediocrity and despair.

When Michael J. Fox gets involved in his time machine adventure, he gets entangled in the lives of his parents when they are still in high school, on the very day that they met. And they met in a curious way. His clumsy, painfully shy father was hit by a car in front of his mother's house while lurking there, trying to catch a glimpse of her. The mother took him into her house to nurse him back to health and fell in love with him out of pity. When Michael J. Fox arrives a moment before the father, he is hit by the car, and his mother falls in love with him instead.

He now has a very big problem. He has to make his mother fall out of love with him and in love with his geeky future father or he isn't even going to exist. He accomplishes this one evening when his mother is being molested in the front seat of a car by the town bully. Fox goads his father into rescuing her, in the process of which, the father knocks out the bully with a lucky punch and his mother is saved. The mother immediately transfers her love from her future son to her new hero.

Now that in itself is profound because it says that a love inspired by heroic deeds is stronger than a love brought on by pity. But there's more. When Fox gets back to the present, everything about the lives of his family has miraculously changed. His mother is no longer an alcoholic, his father is a big success and a real dude, and they're living in a magnificent, creatively appointed house—all because of that one change in the father's character.

The important bit of wisdom has to do with the incredible difference one courageous act can make in our lives. Standing up to that bully had an extraordinary and profound effect far into the future. We encounter numerous such challenges and opportunities to show our courage every day: the phone call we're afraid to make to ask for a date or a job, the little acts of courage that could profoundly and irrevocably change the rest of our lives. That's also very useful to know.

One final example. In a fairy tale called *Aga Baba*, a young hero on an important adventure stops to rest at a witch's house. The witch tries to delay him by asking him some intriguing but difficult questions, like: "What is truth?" "Does the universe ever end?" and so on.

The wise young hero looks at her and says, "Shut up and get me something to eat."

The wisdom in this story is simple enough: Beware of imponderables when action is necessary. Don't while away your days worrying about infinity or other unanswerable questions when you should be out looking for a job.

So there you have three important bits of advice: Change yourself and you change your destiny; little acts of courage performed today can have exponential effects on the rest of your life; and beware of imponderables when action is necessary.

And here again it's accumulative, each story contributing a little bit more of the hidden truth. When you've got a hundred such bits of wisdom working for you, all you have to do is get up in the morning and you'll know exactly what to do and how to do it.

So that's how the great stories do their work. They stimulate our imaginations and give us little tastes of paradise. These trigger fantasies, which lead us to desires for actions in the real world. Then, as we pursue these goals, the stories guide us through the passages using meaningful connections, each story revealing a little bit more of the truth.

CHAPTER 6

How This Natural Storymaking Process Was Cut Off

So, what happened to this natural storymaking process? Why was it cut off? Why are stories with this kind of power only rarely or accidentally being created?

While I would be the last person to attack the virtues of the written word, the fact remains that when these old great stories were finally written down, a serious thing happened. They stopped changing and evolving. They stopped growing. This natural creative process came to a dead stop.

I have a copy of *Grimm's Fairy Tales* on my bookshelf. The stories in that book haven't changed in well over a hundred years, not since the Brothers Grimm took them out of the oral tradition and wrote them down. The Old Testament on my bookshelf hasn't changed in over twenty-five hundred years. In time these stories lose their relevance and their effectiveness. They still contain the same wisdom they always did, if you take the trouble to hunt for it, but the average person no longer sees their relevance because their metaphors haven't been kept up-to-date. So they don't get the message. The knowledge they need to make these journeys is lost to them.

If *Cinderella*, for instance, had remained in the oral tradition, it would have evolved into a modern, contemporary story like *Pretty Woman*, and people could see more easily that it related to their lives.

Now, it is in fact true that this evolutionary process continues on today in a modified form. There have been dozens of different written versions of *Cinderella*, and Hollywood is constantly remaking or updating old movies, many of which are based on stories that originally came out of the oral tradition, but this represents only minor increments of change. And furthermore, because of Hollywood's bias toward entertainment only, the stories are corrupted rather than advanced, their hidden wisdom polluted or leached out rather than enhanced or intensified. As a result they lose most of their power and meaning. Disney's *Snow White*, *Pinocchio*, *Aladdin*, and *Beauty and the Beast* seem like happy exceptions.

So if the natural creative storymaking process is not in fact dead, it is very nearly so and desperately needs resuscitation.

CHAPTER 7

How Stories Are Created Today

Now let's look at how stories are created today by individual authors and why, except in extremely rare cases, they tend to have no real power.

Since the old great stories were being created in a wholly natural and instinctive way, there was no need for anyone to consciously understand exactly what they were or how and why they were being created. They were useful or pleasant to retell and that's all that mattered. There was no need to understand the principles and the principles were not known. That only became important after individuals began to make up stories on their own and write them down.

When you create a story consciously, that's when a knowledge of principles and a good story model become critical. The principles guide you toward the real needs of the audience and line you up with the creative unconscious so you're both shooting for the same thing. And the story model acts as a conductor drawing the hidden wisdom to the surface.

Without a good story model, you can't get unconscious cooperation and support. And without unconscious cooperation and support, you can't get that vital information programmed into your stories and they won't have any real power or meaning. Whatever your story model is, that's your limitation. You can't rise above it. If you think a story is only "boy meets girl," "finding a treasure," or "solving a crime"—or worse yet, just character and structure, conflict and turning points—that's all you're going to get because that's all you're going to be shooting for. Every idea will be pressed into that one mold. The better your story model, the better your story because you can access and accommodate more of that vital information.

Without solid principles and a knowledge of what stories really are, you're like a sailor who sets out to sea without rudder or compass and has almost no chance of reaching his destination. It becomes a strictly hit-and-miss, random process. And that's basically the situation we have today, a lot of mildly entertaining but empty stories being created by this random process because we only have these specialized and polarized story models that are based on the few significant dimensions that have been discovered. The stories they produce don't make a psychological connection, they lack hidden wisdom and truth, and they aren't really that entertaining. The few exceptions become instant superhits.

So what's the real bottom line? The bottom line is that you have six billion people in the world who, from early childhood to old age, have a desperate need for real stories which is not being met. The old great stories are not being replaced. The intelligence and wisdom needed to guide us through these passages isn't getting through to us. We're cut off from it. And the world is in desperate trouble.

On the PBS series they did together, Bill Moyers asked Joseph Campbell if we can get along without myth. And Campbell replied very emphatically, "No we can't. All you have to do is read the papers. It's a mess."

There is simply no way the current Hollywood system of development, which is built on misconceptions about story and entertainment and what the public really wants and needs, can ever meet this need. Literally thousands of screenplays and story ideas are cooked up and submitted to Hollywood each year. Two thousand or more are actively developed; four hundred or so are actually produced; and fewer than ten, in my opinion, are worth seeing. The same is true of novels and plays.

Something is obviously wrong.

What is wrong is you have an entire industry manufacturing something it doesn't understand. If they did that in Detroit, manufactured cars without a clue to their real purpose, it would be a joke. The motor would be in the back seat and the wheels would be in the trunk. You'd have chaos.

In any case, if you're a storymaker, don't be intimidated by the numbers I quoted above. The vast majority of the screenplays and stories that are submitted to Hollywood are created by complete novices—mariners who are hopelessly lost at sea without rudder or compass. If you came to this book to get those principles and tools, I am going to put that knowledge into your hands and give you a realistic chance of realizing your storymaking dreams.

My solution involves teaching you how to emulate this natural creative storymaking process and put all of your conscious and unconscious creative powers into your work. I do this, first of all, by teaching you the nature and purpose of story. This is the compass that will orient you toward the real needs and desires of the audience. And secondly, by showing you how to use the creative process, the language of metaphor, and a sophisticated story model to bring this hidden truth to the surface. All without compromising in any way the things you really want to write about.

There are four great secrets hidden in this book. And this is the first: The author of those old great stories is inside you. And I don't mean that figuratively, I mean it literally. The intelligence and wisdom that created those old great stories is inside you. You can get in touch with that source and make that precious knowledge and the power that goes with it come alive in your work. And, if you combine that power with a contemporary realism and character, you can create superpowerful stories that have a significant impact on the world. And you can make yourself very successful and perhaps even whole in the process.

PART TWO

THE SECRET LANGUAGE OF GREAT STORIES

CHAPTER 8

THE METAPHORS

Metaphor is the symbolic language that expresses the unconscious hidden wisdom. And we'll use that hidden truth as a reference point.

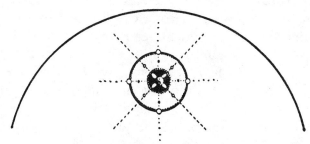

You remember I said in Chapter 2 that this hidden truth exists as raw energy, and in order to be communicated to consciousness, it has to be translated into visual images—that is, the characters, places, actions, and objects that you actually encounter in a great story. These visual images are called **metaphors**. Metaphor literally means "to carry over," to substitute one thing for another. To describe one thing by means of another. To describe something that is unknown by the use of things that are known. In this case, to use everyday, visible, real things to describe (or express) these invisible, unconscious energies. And this is the second great secret revealed in this work, namely, that metaphors are made of real things that have been taken apart and artistically rearranged to represent these hidden truths.

For example, a certain Chinese dragon which represents some of these unconscious creative energies is made up of bits and pieces from a variety of other real animals. It has the head of a camel, the horns of a deer, the eyes of a rabbit, the teeth of a lion, the ears of a cow, the neck of a snake, the belly of a frog, the scales of a carp, the claws of a hawk, and the padded palms of a tiger.

Similarly, Superman, Dracula, the time machine in *Back to the Future*, and the Hindu god Shiva are all made up of bits and pieces of a variety of other real things that have been taken apart and artistically treated.

Superman wears a blue leotard and tights, a red cape, swim trunks, and boots—all common everyday things put together in an unusual, rarely seen color combination. And that gives them their otherworldly character. He has X-ray vision. X-rays and vision are two real things that are combined here artistically to create a superhuman power. He can fly faster than a speeding bullet, leap over tall buildings in a single bound, and he has superhuman strength. Flying, leaping, and strength are all common everyday things which in this case have been greatly exaggerated—exaggeration being one of the important artistic treatments that help to reveal the hidden truth.

Dracula has a serpent's fangs. He sucks blood like a vampire bat. He can transform himself into a wolf or a bat. He sleeps in a coffin filled with Transylvanian dirt. His eyes turn a lurid red when he is excited or angry. He can only be killed if a wooden stake is driven through his heart or if he's exposed to the sun. All everyday things in a unique combination.

The time machine in *Back to the Future* is a DeLorean car and a unique collection of artistically treated real parts. The Hindu god Shiva wears a crown of skulls and is associated with the linga (phallus) and fire. All everyday things.

The real things that create these metaphors already have meanings attached to them which are the result of long association. And when they are artistically treated, they bring these qualities along. Fire means everything fire is and does. Fire is a source of light and heat that can be either creative or destructive. When fire is used metaphorically, as a symbol, it can mean any and all of these things. If you understand the nature of fire, you understand its symbolic meaning.

Fire is one of the attributes of Shiva and this signifies that Shiva can be both creative and destructive. He also wears a crown of skulls. The long association with skulls is death. Many skulls mean many deaths, many deaths mean many rebirths. The phallus (linga) is a sign of masculine sexuality and creativity, and so on. When you understand all of Shiva's qualities, and you see them in the context of a story, you can make meaningful connections and discover these dimensions in yourself.

Water means what water is and does. It is the source and matrix of life. Vampire bats suck blood. Lambs are meek. Fangs are venomous. Spiders are patient. Rabbits are prolific. Doors separate chambers. Keys open doors.

These are the things the creative unconscious has to work with. That's all that is available. And since nothing in the real world can by itself adequately express or represent these powerful unconscious energies, it has to utilize what is available and take a little bit from here and a little bit from there and fashion it into a new form which reflects as nearly as possible the hidden secrets.

The unique combination of these real things when brought together creates the characters, gods, Shangri-las, haunted houses, and real people which express different attributes and dimensions of the hidden energies. The natural world is taken apart and rearranged to reveal the supernatural, unconscious, hidden world.

So when the creative unconscious self wishes to express some aspect of itself, through stories created in an oral tradition, it takes a little bit of this real thing and a little bit of that real thing and artistically treats it using those curious tendencies of the mind we spoke of in Chapter 3, which are really the artistic tools of the imagination. It idealizes this, exaggerates that, minimizes or vilifies something else, takes this apart and recombines it, keeps this and discards that, and so on.

In Milton's *Paradise Lost*, when Satan is on his way to Paradise to corrupt Adam and Eve, he passes through the gates of Hell, which are so huge that their hinges create thunder and lightning storms when they move. By exaggerating the size of the gates and hinges, minimizing the size of the thunderstorm, and reversing their relative sizes, a whole new world is created—a door between Heaven and Hell, a door between our higher and lower selves.

In *David and Goliath* and *Jack and the Beanstalk*, the size of the adversaries is greatly exaggerated and fearsome giants are created. In the movie *Jaws* the size of the man-eating white shark is exaggerated. These alterations create a certain affect. The new relative sizes and equations have special significance. They correspond to certain psychological states and provoke emotional responses from which meaningful connections can be made.

For example, the human mind has the unique ability to go back into the past or to look into the future. And if you were the creative unconscious mind and you wanted to express those abilities to consciousness using the visual metaphors of story, how would you do that?

The stories evolved by the Greeks used Prometheus and his brother Epimetheus. Prometheus in Greek means "forethought"; Epimetheus, "afterthought."

Prometheus stole fire from the gods and gave it to human beings. And for this he was severely punished. The god Zeus had him chained between two great rocks and every morning a large eagle came and gnawed on his liver. During the night, the liver would heal. But then the following day the bird would return and gnaw on his liver again.

It doesn't take a great stretch of the imagination to realize that forethought, the ability to look ahead into the future, had a major role to play in humans' discovery of fire. It would simply not have been possible without it. Forethought was an important evolutionary step. But certain unpleasant side effects evolved along with it, among them, worry. The ability to look ahead means that you can anticipate certain unpleasant possibilities in the future and worry about them. A bird gnawing on the liver (the seat of anxiety) is an excellent way of expressing how worry behaves. But even serious worries will heal or be resolved during the night. But then when you wake up again the next morning, you look toward the future again and there are new things to worry about. The bird returns. The truth hidden in the Prometheus stories reveals not only the nature and importance of forethought but also the relation of forethought to worry and the nature of worry itself.

What about Epimetheus? Afterthought. We can use this ability to go back into the past and correct mistakes, do psychological repairs. This is what psychoanalysis is all about.

And how might you express these abilities in a contemporary story using modern metaphors? Try *Back to the Future*, Part I, where the time machine is used to express these same psychoanalytic abilities. And because the time machine can go either into the future or into the past, it is a perfect modern replacement for the metaphors of old that expressed these mental abilities—forethought and afterthought.

In any case, using this extraordinary device (a souped-up DeLorean sports car), Michael J. Fox goes back into the past and identifies and corrects a serious weakness in his father, which brings about a profound change in the present. That's psychoanalysis. The story is a little road map of these unique mental abilities. And because the story makes that psychological connection—whether done intentionally or not—is why, in my opinion, the film was so successful.

The haunted house story is another modern way of expressing that same psychological model. The house is a perfect metaphor for the human mind, because the human mind, like the house, is a dwelling occupied by living beings. The haunted house, then, is an excellent metaphor of a haunted mind. How do you cure a haunted mind? Well, that's the mind's psychoanalytic ability again. You have to look back into the past and understand the cause of the mental disturbance (the haunting), which is often the result of some traumatically repressed natural instinct crying out for release. And you have to identify the cause of the repression before you can effect a release. The ghost doing the haunting is usually the result of the murder of some innocent person in the house. Murder is an excellent way of metaphorically expressing acts of repression. In order to bring about the release of the ghost, the new occupant of the haunted house has to track down and identify the killer (repressor) of the innocent victim (repressed virtue). Once the killer is identified and punished, the ghost is released and mental health is restored.

CHAPTER 9

THE ARCHETYPES

Great stories, then, are complex metaphors, their different characters, places, actions, and objects all reflecting different aspects of this hidden, inner truth. And if you analyze hundreds of great stories, certain patterns begin to emerge. These patterns are called **archetypes**.

Archetype means "basic form" or "first type." So these basic forms become an intermediate stage between the raw energy of the hidden truth and the metaphors. It is a first model from which the metaphors will spring. All of the symbolic elements, in fact, that we are going to meet in story represent one of these basic psychological forces—these archetypes.

For instance, let us say that the father figure is one of these archetypes. Then Obi-Wan Kenobi (Alec Guinness) in *Star Wars* (an obvious father figure) is a metaphor of that archetype. Jor-El (Marlon Brando) in *Superman,* Jack Warden in *The Verdict*, and Mufasa in *The Lion King* are other examples. They are all metaphors of that father figure archetype.

The model created from these archetypal elements or patterns is, in effect, a rough sketch of the hidden truth. And that's the third great secret, that a sophisticated model of the hidden truth can be made by analyzing the patterns found in great stories. These patterns are the source of *meaningful connections*, and seeing these patterns is the breaking of the story code.

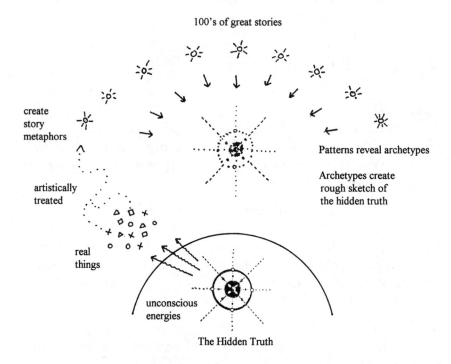

100's of great stories

create
story
metaphors

Patterns reveal archetypes

Archetypes create
rough sketch of
the hidden truth

artistically
treated

real
things

unconscious
energies

The Hidden Truth

To summarize: The hidden truth, utilizing the qualities of real things that have been artistically treated, expresses itself in great stories as metaphors. The patterns found in these great stories can therefore be used to create an archetypal model which is, in effect, a rough sketch of this hidden truth. This rough sketch is our psychological model. Later, when we are working with the creative storymaking process, we will use this model as a reference to help us communicate effectively with the creative unconscious source.

PART THREE

THE NEW STORY MODEL

CHAPTER 10

THE HIDDEN TRUTH

I've divided the study of the hidden truth into four parts:

1. The Storywheel

2. The Golden Paradigm

3. The Story Focus

4. The Sugar Coat

The study of the **storywheel** is the study of all of the cycles of change and growth that we experience from birth to zenith and from zenith to death (or nadir).

zenith

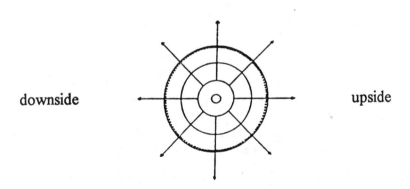

downside   upside

nadir

Every great story, ancient or modern, has a place on this wheel, and when you bring all of the different types of story together in this way, you begin to see how they are all really connected and have a common purpose, namely: they all obviously have something to do with guiding us to higher states of being.

The study of the **Golden Paradigm** is the study of one of these cycles, one of these passages. It is the most important part of our model because it contains the basic patterns and blueprints that are repeated in all the stages of the storywheel, like a genetic code.

We use this design to illustrate the Golden Paradigm:

paradise

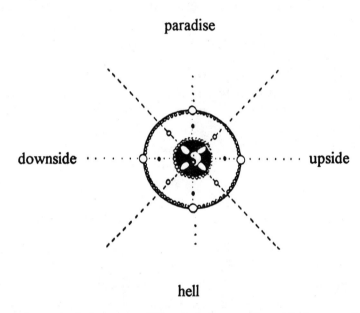

downside   upside

hell

And each one of the ascending and descending circles on the storywheel represents one of these Golden Paradigm models.

Metaphors that describe the Golden Paradigm are also, in effect, describing the human psyche, the psyche being that part of the human mind that has been mapped. The Golden Paradigm is a way of looking at the psyche. It is a dynamic model of the psyche, showing its structures and dimensions and how these structures and dimensions interact, evolve, and are transformed.

The third part of our model is the **story focus**. Each great story, as we've been saying, reveals a small part of the hidden truth, a little bit more of the Golden Paradigm. The stories build up and reveal the paradigm, and the paradigm repeats itself and creates the storywheel.

The Iliad is a good story to illustrate the relationship of the Golden Paradigm to the story focus. *The Iliad* is really a whole, big story concerning the seduction of Helen of Troy by the Trojan, Paris, and the war that was fought by the Greeks to get her back. The focus of that *whole story* is a single incident, the argument between Achilles and Agamemnon and its consequences in the ninth year of the war. The *whole story* is told in the context of this one dispute. The study of the Golden Paradigm is the study of the structures, dimensions, and dynamics of this larger, *whole story* (frame or backstory) while the study of the *story focus* is the study of the structures, dimensions, and dynamics of the little story itself, that is, the dispute between Agamemnon and Achilles.

The fourth and final part of our study will be the **sugar coat**, which refers to the entertainment dimensions that help to attract interest in the story and also to camouflage and conceal its hidden secrets.

We'll begin with the Golden Paradigm, the metaphors that describe the human psyche.

CHAPTER 11

THE GOLDEN PARADIGM

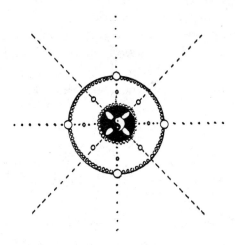

Because the transformations that take place during these passages
(or cycles) are psychic transformations, the Golden Paradigm is a
model of the human psyche. It is a model of our conscious and
unconscious minds in transition. It will show us the relationship
between the conscious and the unconscious minds:

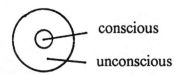

and their different dimensions:

It will show us how these dimensions are organized, how they

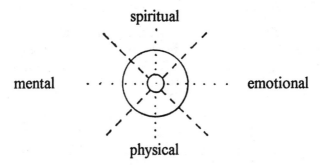

function, and how they interact. And finally the model will show us how unconscious "potential" energy is transformed by certain actions into energy that can be consciously used and controlled:

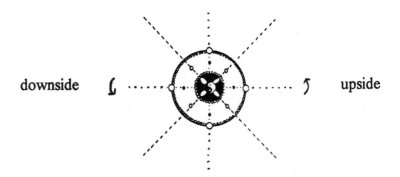

There are four types of metaphors or archetypes that describe the Golden Paradigm. The first are the metaphors and archetypes that describe the different dimensions of our conscious and unconscious selves. These are the **character archetypes**, the major players and heroes of story.

The second type of metaphor describes the **organization of the psyche**. These archetypal patterns reveal how the mind functions, how the conscious and unconscious minds relate to each other and communicate, and how the creative unconscious archetypes interact: their relative hierarchy, rivalry, powers, and goals.

The third type of metaphor reveals **the path**. These are the actions and plots of story that reveal the creative actions and tasks which are necessary to awaken and release the extraordinary powers that bring about the shifts to higher consciousness.

The fourth type of metaphor describes the archetypes which reveal the vast, lost or unrealized potential. These are the **marvelous** and the **terrible elements**, the magic objects and powers in a story. Psychologically, these are the building blocks of higher consciousness.

Our Conscious and Unconscious Selves

In our model, as I just indicated, I illustrate the relationship between the conscious and unconscious minds as a small circle surrounded by a larger circle:

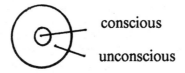

In great stories the pattern that reveals this relationship is the contrasting of two worlds—a familiar, known, everyday world and an unfamiliar, remote, mysterious, dark, or supernatural world. In *The Wizard of Oz*, the known (conscious) world of Kansas is contrasted with the strange and fantastic (unconscious) world of Oz. In *Dances with Wolves* and *Pocahontas*, the civilized world or a fort belonging to the new Americans is contrasted with the natural wilderness of the Native Americans. In *Peter Pan*, it's London and Never-Never Land. In *E.T.*, *Contact*, and *Armageddon*, it's the Earth and outer space. In *Alien*, it's the control room and the remote, less familiar parts of the spaceship. In *Jurassic Park*, it's the compound and the rest of the park.

These contrasts do not have to involve something that is fantastic or supernatural. It can be the juxtaposition of things in the real world: a contrast between the regular living quarters of a house and a spooky basement or attic; the everyday world of the detective and the shady underworld. In *Chinatown*, it's the everyday world of J.J. Gittes and the San Fernando Valley. In *Titanic*, it's the upper decks contrasted by the bowels of the ship, and later, after the iceberg, the sinking ship contrasted by the open sea. In *Jaws*, it's an island surrounded by the sea. The sea is an excellent metaphor for the unconscious because, like the unconscious, the ocean is a vast, mostly hidden domain that is teeming with mysterious life forms. And the island is an excellent metaphor for the conscious mind, which is very much like an island surrounded by an unconscious sea.

This is a very important pattern, and you will find it, in some form or other, in every great story.

The Character Archetypes

There are nine character archetypes or major players in our study—the Ego/Hero, the Spiritual, the Mental, the Emotional, the Physical, the Anima/Animus, the Trickster, the Threshold Guardian, and the Shadow.

The **ego/hero** is the archetype of the conscious self, and all of the other characters in the story are metaphors representing the archetypes of the creative unconscious self.

To recall an earlier quote from Joseph Campbell, "Myths and dreams are the manifestations in image form of all of the energies of the body, moved by the organs, in conflict with each other." The archetypes of the creative unconscious self are the personifications of these organic energies in conflict.

We illustrate the different levels of the unconscious self by adding spokes or rays which emanate from the small, conscious center:

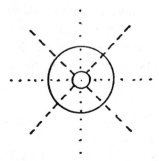

The basic divisions we're using to describe these unconscious archetypes (these energies in conflict) are the four essential dimensions of our selves, namely: the physical, the emotional, the mental, and the spiritual, so we will have archetypes that describe the operating energies of the physical self, the emotional self, the mental self, and the spiritual self:

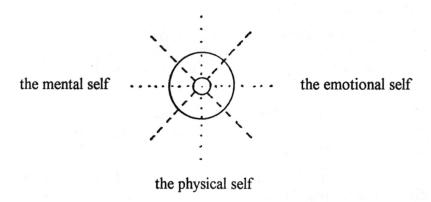

I call these archetypes the **spiritual archetypes**, the **mental archetypes**, the **emotional archetypes**, and the **physical archetypes**. In great stories, these are the forces of assistance and resistance—the allies, enemies, and other important characters that confront and surround the hero and act as antagonists or guides.

The **anima/animus archetypes** are the love interests in a story. They act as contacts and go-betweens and are the ego/hero's guide to the soul. I illustrate these archetypes in our model as the flower petals linking the conscious center to the surrounding unconscious:

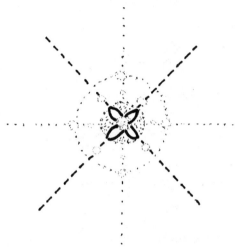

The **tricksters** are the troublemakers that goad the conscious archetypes forward when they get stuck. I illustrate them as the small circles imbedded in the lighter spokes.

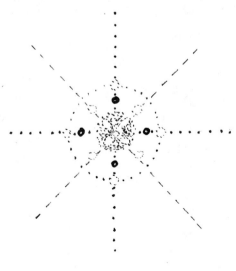

The **threshold guardians** act as obstacles and barriers. They stand in the way of the conscious archetypes and are there to verify their preparedness and test their resolve. I illustrate them as the larger circles imbedded in the bolder spokes:

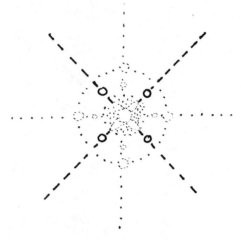

Each of these major sets of archetypes has a male and a female aspect, which can be either positive or negative. By "positive" I mean favoring the creative goals of the higher, spiritual self, and by "negative" I mean favoring the creative interests and goals of the lower, primordial self. I illustrate these attributes as yin and yang, the Chinese symbol of opposites:

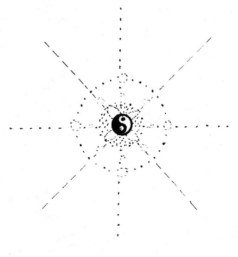

We experience these character archetypes, as we do all of the archetypes, in four ways: We experience them in story and in dreams, but we also experience them psychologically and in real life. In real life, we experience them as the different roles we're called upon to play. Psychologically, we experience them as feelings, thoughts, physical sensations, desires, fantasies, mental images, and so on. Feelings of aggression, desire, and hunger, for instance, are all expressions of the lower, instinctual, physical self.

The **shadow** is all of the repressed elements of our psychic selves that got stuffed into the trunks of the personal unconscious. These elements can be either spiritual, emotional, mental, or physical, conscious or unconscious, positive or negative.

In Freudian psychology, these repressed elements are all there is to the unconscious. After Carl Jung described the collective, archetypal unconscious we all share in common, he renamed the repressed elements the shadow. We indicate the shadow in our model as the shadowy ring that surrounds consciousness:

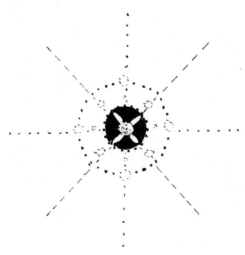

In story and dreams, these repressed elements become demons, mummies, ghosts, and archvillains.

Communication

The conscious and unconscious minds work very closely together. Information passes easily between the two worlds. The unconscious mind is omnipresent. It knows all and sees all that is happening within and around the conscious mind. The unconscious mind communicates with consciousness by means of insights, feelings, premonitions, mental images, intuitions, dreams, and so on. They are visitors into consciousness. So in story we see these communications expressed as visitors or messengers from the remote or supernatural regions: E.T., Superman, and the aliens in *Independence Day* are visitors from outer space; the Terminator comes from our own future; George Burns in *Oh, God!* comes from Heaven; the Devil in *The Exorcist* and the dark forces in *Ghost* come from Hell; Peter Pan visits from Never-Never Land.

The conscious mind can communicate with the unconscious mind as well. We do this when we use our creative imaginations, when we ask ourselves questions, say our prayers, meditate, create fantasies, or dream. When we dream, the conscious mind ventures into the strange and fantastic world of the unconscious. In great stories, we see this enacted as the hero venturing into these other worlds: Jack scurries up the beanstalk to the giant's house in the clouds; Jacob climbs the ladder into Heaven; Alice tumbles into a rabbit hole and ends up in Wonderland; Dorothy rides a tornado into Oz; Pinocchio journeys into the ocean and ends up in the belly of a whale; J.J. Gittes heads for the San Fernando Valley; Sigourney Weaver searches the remote recesses of the spaceship seeking the alien.

This is another extremely important pattern.

CHAPTER 12

INNER CONFLICT

Why are these creative unconscious energies in conflict? You can get a clue to that if you study our evolutionary development, whereby we evolved from reptiles to mammals to primates to early humans to Homo sapiens (man the wise). Each new development of the brain superseded the previous one. The physical, instinctual reptilian brain was covered over by the emotional, mammalian brain, or limbic system, and the mammalian brain was covered over by the thinking, human brain, or neo-cortex. There's a spiritual brain in there somewhere, but it hasn't been located yet.

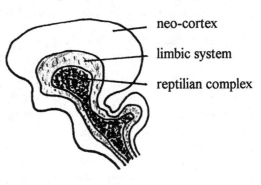

neo-cortex

limbic system

reptilian complex

You can see this development in the human fetus, in animated time-lapse photography, where the later, younger brains clearly seem to be overlaying the earlier, older ones. The older, lower forces are, in effect, being overthrown by the younger, higher forces.

Somewhere along the line, the ego, the center of the conscious mind, was developed to act as an administrator and mediator of all of these forces. There's been a struggle for power going on ever since. And the main objective of the principal opposing forces (the spiritual and the physical) has been to influence and control the conscious element (the ego) and use it as a power-releasing, consciousness-building resource.

Now, if you were the creative unconscious self and you wanted to express these evolutionary ideas to consciousness using metaphors—real things that have been artistically treated and arranged into stories—how would you do that? Two stories which illustrate this basic evolutionary situation come to mind—the Greek myth of the battle of the Titans, and the Bible story about the battle between God and Satan.

In the battle of the Titans, the newer, younger, Olympian gods, led by Zeus, take on and overthrow the older, Titanic gods led by Cronus. Zeus wins and becomes king of the gods and Cronus is sealed up in Tartarus, the Greek underworld. That is a perfect metaphor for what I have been describing—newer, younger, more powerful brain functions superseding older, lower forces.

In the Bible story, the same basic battle is fought between God and Satan. Satan loses and is condemned to Hades. As part of Satan's counterattack, he turns himself into a serpent and goes up to the Garden of Eden to corrupt God's new favorites, Adam and Eve. He tempts them with an apple that can give them some of God's great power. They break God's law and are driven out of Paradise.

In this story, God represents, of course, the higher spiritual self, and Satan the lower, superseded, physical self which is shut up in the underworld. Adam and Eve represent the conscious self, the ego. This is made clear by the fact that they are naming things. That's one of the things the conscious mind does, it gives names to things. And finally, the snake is a perfect metaphor of the lower, physical self, which is, in fact, a reptile brain, the source of our most basic physical instincts, appetites, and drives.

The two important structural patterns revealed by these stories show that the conscious and unconscious energies are organized in a **hierarchy**—the physical, instinctual self has been superseded by the higher self, and they're in conflict. There is a **rivalry** between them. The spiritual dimension is above, the physical dimension is below, and the conscious element, which they are both trying to influence, is caught in the middle.

You see this hierarchy very clearly in the two stories. Heaven is above, Hell is below, and the Garden of Eden is in the middle.

Mount Olympus is above, Tartarus is below, and the Earth is in the middle. The physical and spiritual sides of our nature are in conflict and our conscious selves are caught in the middle.

You see this relationship in the movie *Ghost*. The conscious world is the real world, and when the good die, they leave the real world and rise up to the spiritual light. When the evil ones die, they are dragged down below into the dark underworld. Light, by the way, is a metaphor for consciousness. Bright or white light is associated with spiritual or higher consciousness, and darkness belongs to the lower, instinctual consciousness. The powers of darkness.

In stories, the most frequent manifestation of the rivalry between the light and dark sides of our nature is the struggle between good and evil. These are all very persistent patterns in story with which I'm sure everyone is familiar.

CHAPTER 13

THE EGO/HERO ARCHETYPE

I call the ego's participation in the cycles of transformation a "passage," and the hero's participation in these cycles his or her "journey" or "adventure." Like the storywheel, these cycles and passages have a positive and negative side, an **upside** and a **downside**. I illustrate this in our model as arrows going counterclockwise around the Golden Paradigm:

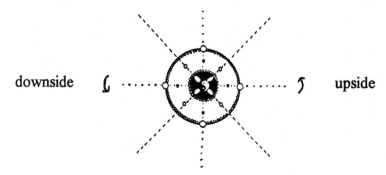

downside   upside

To function properly as the center of consciousness, the ego has to be initiated and strengthened at every step. The actions of the hero show the ego the way through this **initiation** process.

As Joseph Campbell explains, "The standard path of the mythological adventure of the hero is a magnification of the formula represented in the rites of passage: separation–initiation–return, which might be named the nuclear unit of the monomyth."

What Jung and Campbell discovered that was so remarkable was a connection between certain patterns in myths and dreams and the rites of passage of primitive tribes, the common purpose being to guide the initiate to higher states of maturity and awareness, that is, to a greater share of consciousness. The separation–initiation–return pattern is, in fact, innate. And great stories bring these patterns to consciousness.

In his book *The Origins and History of Consciousness*, Erich Neumann writes:

> "Individual consciousness passes through the same archetypal stages of development that marked the history of human consciousness as a whole. The stages begin and end with the symbol of the Uroboros, or tail-eating serpent; the intermediary stages are projected in the universal myths of the World Creation, the Great Mother, the Separation of the World Parents, the Birth of the Hero, the Slaying of the Dragon, the Rescue of the Captive, and the Transformation and Deification of the Hero. The hero throughout this sequence is the evolving ego consciousness."

Like the other major archetypes, the ego/hero has a male and female aspect, which can be either positive or negative. I call the positive aspect the **nascent ego** and the negative aspect the **holdfast**. In our story model, I call the nascent ego the **hero** and the holdfast the **antihero**. The hero can be either male or female, positive or negative: Indiana Jones is a positive male hero; Sigourney Weaver in *Alien*, Demi Moore in *G.I. Jane*, and Mulan are positive female heroes. Macbeth is a negative, male antihero; Scarlett O'Hara is a negative female antihero.

The Nascent Ego

Nascent means "about to be born." The nascent ego is the conscious element on the upside of the cycle that is about to be awakened and transformed into hero consciousness (a mature ego). It is the conscious desire to participate in this consciousness-building process. It is the desire to grow, the desire to do something meaningful with our lives, the desire to make a contribution and reach our full potential. It is the part of us that recognizes problems, accepts responsibility, resists temptation, and shares good fortune. It is the unselfish, positive side of the ego.

In real life, it's anyone who is about to take part in some meaningful transformation. It's real heroes like Lech Walesa in Poland, Vaclav Havel in Czechoslovakia, or Martin Luther King in the U.S. when they are about to risk everything and sacrifice everything to bring about positive, meaningful change.

In story, it is the potential heroes at the beginning of the story before they have proven themselves. It is Luke Skywalker in *Star Wars* before he meets Obi-Wan Kenobi. It is Rocky while he's still wandering the streets. It's Dorothy in Kansas before she gets to Oz. It's Belle at the beginning of Disney's *Beauty and the Beast*, hoping there's more than "this provincial life." It's Jodie Foster in *The Silence of the Lambs* before she is influenced by Hannibal Lecter (Anthony Hopkins), and Will Shakespeare in *Shakespeare In Love*, before he meets Viola.

The audience identifies with the hero and the hero draws them into the experience and guides them through the paradigm. The truer the hero is to the ego archetype, the stronger the identification of the recipient of the story. And, if the hero is a role model, someone we want to be like, then the story can have a powerful influence on our lives.

The Holdfast

Psychologically, the holdfast is just the opposite. Whereas the nascent ego is a positive impulse that propels us forward toward positive actions or change, the holdfast is the impulse to "hold on" to what we have and resist change. It is the desire to stay in a safe, comfortable place or keep everything exactly as it is. We experience this aspect of the holdfast first as the infant who doesn't want to give up its mother's breast, or the two-year-old tyrants who throw tantrums when they don't get their way, or the child who doesn't want to grow up. This is the negative, selfish side of the ego, the egotistical side that has given the word "ego" a bad name, as in egotistic or egomaniacal.

Dustin Hoffman in *Kramer vs. Kramer* is a holdfast. He doesn't want to grow up. The three men in *Three Men and a Baby* are holdfasts. They don't want to give up their playboy-bachelor lifestyles and take on the responsibilities of a wife and family.

The holdfast is also the part of us that gives in to temptation, the part that seeks to give pleasure to the senses, the part that can be taken over by the dark side. It is the impulse to do something that is essentially self-destructive. This is Adam and Eve, Scarlett O'Hara, Othello, and Macbeth. This is also King David after he meets Bathsheba, Samson after he meets Delilah, William Hurt after he meets Kathleen Turner in *Body Heat*, and Michael Douglas in *Fatal Attraction* and *Basic Instinct*.

A final characteristic of the holdfast is the will to power and insatiable greed. This is the materialistic, power-hungry, tyrannical side of our natures, the side that wants to possess everything it desires, without limit, and control everything it needs. This is Johnny Friendly, the Lee J. Cobb character in *On the Waterfront*, the corrupt union boss who will do anything to hold on to his power. This is Captain Bligh in *Mutiny on the Bounty*, Macbeth, Little Caesar, and Michael Corleone in *The Godfather*. And this is King Herod in the New Testament. Herod is the classic holdfast. When he hears the prophecy that some recently born child will grow up to replace him as king, he orders all of the infants in his kingdom under two years old to be slaughtered.

When the holdfast is the central character of a story that ends tragically on the downside, like Macbeth or Michael Douglas in *Basic Instinct* or *Fatal Attraction*, that's when I call them antiheroes.

In real life, the tyrannical holdfast is one of the easiest archetypes to spot. This is Hitler, Mussolini, Lenin, Stalin, and Mao Tsetung. This is Erich Honecker in East Germany, Ferdinand Marcos in the Philippines, Manuel Noriega in Panama, or Saddam Hussein in Iraq. But it can be any politician, company president, or petty tyrant that would rather abuse power than give it up.

The Stages of the Passage

I illustrate the passage of the hero and antihero in our model by naming the spokes. The stages on the upside are **separation, initiation, integration,** and **rebirth.**

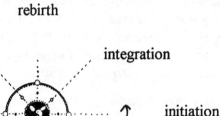

rebirth

integration

initiation

separation

After the ego/hero completes the upside of the passage, he will be drawn into the downside and transformed into a holdfast/anti-hero. Having achieved a great success, the hero will become increasingly reluctant to give up or share any of his newly won power. He will become vulnerable to the seductive powers of the lower self, in the same way that the heroes King David, Samson, and Theseus did.

I call the stages on the downside of the passage: **attachment, regression, alienation,** and **death.**

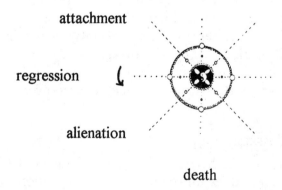

attachment

regression

alienation

death

What the upside is to initiation, the downside is to regression. By regression, we mean "reverting back." We mean shutting down the higher self in favor of the demands of the lower, instinctual self. And we see both initiation and regression in this case as being positive—two phases in the process of transformation.

Here is a quote concerning regression from *A Critical Dictionary of Jungian Analysis*:

> "Jung's attitude toward regression differed markedly from Freud's. For the latter, regression was almost always a negative phenomenon—something to be fought off and overcome. From 1912 onwards, Jung insisted on the therapeutic and personality-enhancing aspects of periods of regression (without denying the harmful nature of prolonged and unproductive regression). Regression may be seen as a period of regeneration prior to subsequent advance."

The ultimate goal of these passages is the creation and expansion of consciousness. The unconscious, according to what we're being told by the archetypal patterns in story, is a pool of potential consciousness. We start off life, as infants, completely unconscious. The fully realized, ultimate states of mind we hope to achieve reside in the unconscious as conscious potential. The hidden truth revealed by story is all about how these unconscious "potential" energies can be awakened and converted into energies and powers that can be consciously administered and controlled. These unconscious, "potential" energies are, however, extremely powerful and have to be carefully regulated and controlled until the ego has been properly prepared and has proven itself capable of handling it. The gauntlet of proof is the passage. To function properly as the center of consciousness, the ego has to be initiated and strengthened at every step. The purpose of story is to guide the ego through these ego-strengthening passages so it can properly administer these powerful, unconscious energies. The actions of the hero in story show the ego the way through this initiation process.

The Garden of Eden story becomes interesting here because it reveals the beginning of the regressive process which results in the higher self being shut down. On the upside of the passage, the hero resists temptation and goes up the ladder. On the downside, the antihero, in this case Adam and Eve, give in to temptation and go down the ladder. When the conscious element gives in to the temptations of the lower self, an alienation from the higher self occurs. And that is the basic situation which exists today— the spiritual self is shut down and the serpent brain is gaining the upper hand. The ego doesn't know what's going on and is in a life-and-death struggle with the lower, physical self, cut off from any real help from above. We see this clearly when we examine all of the physical addictions to sugar, fat, caffeine, nicotine, alcohol, or drugs, which we're fighting because our appetites have gone awry. The higher, spiritual power could easily come to our aid and subdue these addictive physical powers, but it can't turn on the juice unless the ego can handle it. And the ego can't handle it unless it makes these passages and is strengthened. And it doesn't even know it has to do that because it has lost touch with story, the creative unconscious self, and just about every other source of higher wisdom.

CHAPTER 14

THE MARVELOUS AND TERRIBLE ELEMENTS

In order to complete these passages and reach their respective goals, the nascent ego and the holdfast need power. They need the vast unconscious spiritual, mental, emotional, and physical powers that are waiting to be awakened and released. Psychologically, these are the building blocks of consciousness, the energies without which higher states of being cannot be achieved. They could be extraordinary unrealized creative, healing, or intuitive powers, unrealized talent or genius, extraordinary mental, physical, or sexual abilities, a profound capacity to love, the power to influence the world, the power to transcend duality and experience ultimate truth. In real life, they are the power necessary to bring about changes of fortune: the fabulous sums of money needed to make positive and negative things happen, the evidence necessary to prosecute criminals, the terrible weapons necessary to protect your nation or win hot and cold wars—all things which are difficult to realize but without which the problems cannot be overcome, the tasks cannot be accomplished, and the transformations cannot be made.

In great stories, we see these extraordinary powers and potentials expressed as these real things or as fabulous treasures like King Solomon's mines, the Fountain of Youth, the ancient Egyptian *Book of Thoth*, and the Holy Grail. We see them as supernatural powers like invisibility, flying, and X-ray vision, or as secret formulas, magic potions, ultimate weapons, or magic objects like the Ruby Slippers, Aladdin's lamp, a crystal ball, a time machine, and Samson's hair. Or we see them as fantastic places like Camelot, Shangri-la, El Dorado, and the Promised Land; forgotten paradises like the Garden of Eden; or lost kingdoms like Shambhala, Atlantis, and Utopia.

The hero and the holdfast compete for control of these extraordinary powers. In the hands of the hero, they are Excalibur or the Holy Grail, the building blocks of consciousness. In the hands of the self-destructive antihero, they become voodoo dolls, Svengali's hypnotism, or Dracula's addictive fangs. Or they become death stars or doomsday machines, the scourges of humankind.

Joseph Campbell calls these special powers and objects the ultimate boon, Alfred Hitchcock called them the McGuffin, the thing everybody wants. We call them the **marvelous elements** or the **terrible elements.**

Bill Moyers asked Joseph Campbell on the PBS series they did together, "What is Heaven?" And Joseph Campbell answered, "Heaven is a symbolic place. Heaven is no place. These are planes of consciousness or fields of experience potential in the human spirit."

CHAPTER 15

THE ARCHETYPES OF THE CREATIVE UNCONSCIOUS SELF

In order to accomplish the actions necessary to release these marvelous and terrible powers, the nascent ego and the holdfast have to be motivated and prepared. They cannot perform these tasks alone. The help they need comes from the archetypes of the creative unconscious self. These character archetypes act as the custodians of the miraculous powers and hold the keys to their release. In story, they are the major players, the forces of assistance or resistance—the metaphors that personify these organic energies which are in conflict.

The Physical Archetypes

Carl Jung calls the physical, instinctual archetypes of the lower self the Terrible Mother and the Terrible Father. To us they are the **positive** and **negative physical archetypes**. But we sometimes refer to them collectively as the **great snake**, because anatomically it is the **R-complex**, the reptilian brain that controls the lower, physical, animal side of our nature. The lower self is a primordial, earthbound self. It pursues earthly things. And hidden in the matrix of its mysterious and seductive energies are the libido and the id—the source of our most basic instincts, appetites, and drives. These energies are associated with the three lower chakras, the ones that control hunger, sex, and aggression. And these are the energies that have been superseded by the energies of our higher brains and they don't like it. So they compete with the higher self for influence over the conscious element, and when the nascent ego attempts one of these passages, they are the principal resisters of all positive change. Then after the positive ego has been transformed into a holdfast, they are the holdfast's principal supporters, advisers, and guides. They are the negative forces and impulses that seek to control and corrupt us.

In great stories, the metaphors that describe these basic, instinctual energies take a variety of human and animal forms, depending on which aspects of the lower primordial, physical self they are personifying. And like the ego archetype, they can be either masculine or feminine, positive or negative. Technically, they are all negative in that they all serve the interests and objectives of the lower self, but they take a positive form after they have been transformed.

In an ideal, healthy society, our wholesome physical appetites might be personified in story, as they are in the Greek myths, as Eros and Aphrodite, Hecate and Pluto, or Dionysus—the gods of physical love, material wealth, good food and wine. And the aggressive impulses that urge us to seek revenge, seize territory, kill, or go to war might be represented by Ares or Diana, or by the Hindu gods Shiva and Kali.

But in our modern society, we have created another snake, a demonic snake, which is the result of the repression of some of these basic, natural instincts. This is a **shadow** figure, a source of evil—someone or something that has been taken over by the dark side. This is Anthony Hopkins in *The Silence of the Lambs*, the Evil Emperor and Darth Vader in *Star Wars*, the Devil in *The Exorcist*, the terrible mother monster in *Aliens*, Medusa, T-rex and the velociraptors in *Jurassic Park*, or the shark in *Jaws*. And this is Satan, Dracula, and Mr. Big, the evil behind all evils. And this is Nosferatu, the undead. Dracula is Nosferatu. He's dead but he's immortal. You can't get rid of him. Nosferatu is a perfect metaphor for these repressed psychic elements, which are dead (repressed) but not dead. They come back to haunt us. They are the stuff of horror movies and nightmares.

Psychologically, these repressed elements become the negative energies that inspire lust, hatred, anger and greed, acts of aggression, acts of violence and all of the other deadly sins that can overwhelm us and take away our control. In real life, when people are completely taken over by these dark forces they become serious villains, drug lords, and tyrants. Hitler is still, by far, our best example. But Stalin and Idi Amin are right up there, as are the myriad serial killers and psychopaths that plague our real lives.

Complicating the identification of these shadow figures, in real life and story, is the fact that they will hide their true character. Legitimate antagonists do not hide their negative sides, but the shadow does, and that's why the villain in a whodunit usually turns out to be the least likely suspect. He pretends to be all good. A real human being is a complex creature full of contradictions and a mixture of good and bad traits, and can easily become a suspect. Real villains will hide all evil traits, so they'll appear to be too good to be true. In real life, we see this all the time. It's how evil operates: really despicable and corrupt individuals hiding behind virtue or the flag. To advance their political careers, corrupt politicians will conceal all of their negative qualities and say or do anything to get elected. When they get caught, it turns out all they really cared about was money, sex, and power. Honecker in East Germany was apparently such a villain. Tyranny posing as beneficent ruler.

According to Robert McKee, "The worst possible villains are those pretending to be what they despise. Hate posing as love. Vice posing as virtue. Injustice posing as justice."

The neighbors of the Bronx serial killer, Son of Sam, insisted he was the nicest person they ever met. This is how evil operates.

In any event, the shadow has to be resolved first and integrated into our personality before the conscious elements can get back on the right track and proceed with their initiations. And the clear message of story is not to repress these natural instincts but to civilize and transform them, to be their master and not their slave.

In *Sleeping Beauty*, the king does not invite a dark witch named Maleficent to the celebration honoring his daughter's birth. She appears anyway and in her anger puts a serious curse on the young princess and the royal court. The important meaningful connection to be made in this story is that we cannot pick and choose which dimensions of our psychic selves we wish to integrate. They all have to be invited to the party. When the negative energies are repressed or left out, they get nasty. And it always leaves the conscious element seriously threatened, somewhat enchanted or beast-like.

The Emotional Archetypes

The R-complex , as we indicated, was superseded by our emotional brain, the limbic system, and this gave rise to the emotional archetypes, which I call the **positive** and **negative emotional father** and **mother figures**.

By emotional self, I mean our social self and our social feelings. By social feelings I mean the things we feel when we interact socially with other people or as part of a group (that is, love, a sense of duty, camaraderie, empathy, compassion, excitement, anxiety, guilt, etc.). The emotional parent figures are concerned about emotional things, about personal relationships, about the role the hero and the holdfast should play in society.

Unlike the spiritual and physical self, the emotional self does not have an agenda, other than to make the social entity, whatever its mores, function as a harmonious and effective whole. The social entity can be a community, a corporation, an invading army, or a mob, and it can give its allegiance to either positive or negative ideals, to a Hitler or a Christ. Its character is determined by its objectives.

In real life, the positive emotional father and mother figures are guided by the objectives of the higher self. And they are the people who love us, who nurture and protect us, and teach us our social responsibilities. They teach us how to get along with others, how to be good parents, how to love, how to give and receive affection, and how to cooperate with others and share. They give us advice concerning the professions we should choose. They encourage us to be good citizens and work for the common good, admonish us for being selfish, help us work out our social and emotional problems, and give us the social skills we need to achieve our emotional desires and goals. Psychologically, it's all of the inner promptings that guide us in a similar fashion.

In stories, it's the characters that relate to the hero in this same way. In the movie *Mask*, a mother helps her disfigured son make it in the real world. In *Fried Green Tomatoes*, Jessica Tandy uses a story to guide an unhappy housewife back to an understanding of married life. In *Gone with the Wind*, Hattie McDaniel tries unsuccessfully to put Scarlett O'Hara on the right track. In *The Verdict*, Jack Warden helps rehabilitate an emotionally bankrupt ambulance chaser. In *Class Action*, Gene Hackman is a father who is trying to teach his corporation-defending daughter her social responsibility. But it could be any friend, colleague, relative, or stranger that fills that emotional role.

The negative emotional father and mother figures are just the opposite. They are guided by the objectives of the lower self, and teach us prejudice and hatred and intolerance, and criticize all our efforts to develop a genuine social conscience. They believe human beings are basically evil and have to be dominated by the proper iron fist or they will run amok. It's a dog-eat-dog world and we have to accept that. We should be ambitious and ruthless and use any means to become king of the hill. If you fail to reach the top, you will be nothing.

In real life, they are the social forces that helped create Hitler and Charles Manson. They teach us how to lie, how to persuade, and how to get power over others. They teach us how to organize a cult or secret neo-Nazi society. They want you to create an elite cadre of paramilitary followers and become like Genghis Khan. They need you to become like Genghis Khan. They need you to achieve that kind of greatness so you can put the masses under your spell. Psychologically, they are the inner impulses and promptings that encourage or drive us in this direction.

In story, this is Livia in *I Claudius*, a mother who will stop at nothing, including many murders, to see her son Tiberius emperor.

This is also David Copperfield's blackhearted stepfather, and the father who drove his son to suicide in *Dead Poets Society*. It is also Cinderella's stepmother, Mary Tyler Moore in *Ordinary People*, Kate Nelligan in *The Prince of Tides*, and Henry Fonda in *On Golden Pond*.

The Mental Archetypes

The mental archetypes are the denizens of our thinking brain, the neo-cortex. They are our knowledge, our intelligence, our understanding—our ability to reason, to judge, to think creatively, to plot strategies.

And like the emotional self, the mental self doesn't have an agenda. It's neutral. It can serve either master. Wernher von Braun, America's leading rocket scientist for thirty years after World War II (and the father of the German V-2) was just as comfortable working for Hitler as for the United States. If you want to save the world, the mind will help you do that, providing you with a strategy and a master plan. On the other hand, if you want to rob a bank or kill someone, it will help you do that as well. It's a tool. So, in great stories, the metaphors that reveal these archetypes can serve the interests of either the higher or the lower self.

Jung calls the positive male and female mental archetypes the **wise old man** and the **wise old woman**. The negative aspects he calls the **sorcerer** and the **sorceress**. I have adopted these same names.

The positive wise old man and wise old woman possess a special knowledge which can help the hero achieve his goal. This is Yoda in *Star Wars*, the psychiatrist in *Ordinary People*, Whoopi Goldberg in *Ghost*. In the legends of King Arthur, it's the magician, Merlin. Without the power contained in the invincible sword, Excalibur, Arthur cannot unify England and create Camelot. And without Merlin's help, Arthur cannot possess and control the sword.

In fairy tales, it is frequently an animal like the fox. In *The Jungle*

Book, it's the panther, Bagheera. In *The Lion King*, it's the shaman baboon, Rafiki. But it could take the form of a computer or even a wise child, as in the Hindu myth *Parade of Ants*.

In real life, it could be the mentors who influenced Jonas Salk and Albert Einstein, or the advisers who helped the Allied leaders win World War II.

The negative mental helpers, the sorcerer and sorceress, can also take the form of witches, traitors, evil geniuses, wizards, computers, or spies. They have the special knowledge and powers that can undermine the hero and guide him to his doom. This is Iago in *Othello*, and Mephistopheles in *Faust*, who tempts the ill-fated antihero with the power that will bring about the corruption and damnation of his immortal soul.

In real life, it's Machiavelli, Goebbels, and Adolf Eichmann. They show the holdfast how to be a successful tyrant and fight a blitzkrieg war. They concoct the secret formulas, design the death camps, and construct the doomsday machines that will give the holdfast the power to carry out his diabolical schemes.

The Spiritual Archetypes

The spiritual archetypes, which we call the **positive** or **negative spiritual father** and **mother figures,** are the guiding spirits and hidden wisdom of the higher, unbounded, cosmic self. When the nascent ego is ready for its adventure, the energies of the spiritual self are the principal forces trying to bring about that positive change. They are the creative energies that give birth to the psychological impulses that seek to overcome the negative states and reach the higher states of being. They inspire us to seize the day, to be creative and virtuous, courageous and just, to make sacrifices, and to do great things. They are the source of the power that can make or break our lives, and they want us to be liberated and free—to be at one with our selves, our loved ones, our country, our world, our God, and the cosmos. They are the sum and substance of our souls and the guardians of our destiny.

In great stories, as metaphors, these spiritual energies can take many different male and female forms. They can personify all-seeing, all-powerful gods and goddesses like Hera and Zeus, Isis and Osiris, or they can take a mortal form like Alec Guinness in *Star Wars*, Marlon Brando in *Superman*, the mother in *My Left Foot*, who helps nurture the artistic talents of her paraplegic son, Mufasa in *The Lion King*, the wizard and the good witch in *The Wizard of Oz*, and Queen Elizabeth in *Shakespeare In Love*. They can, in fact, be any positive father or mother figure whose main concerns are spiritual matters—i.e., they inspire and help the hero to reach or bring about higher, more desirable states of being.

In real life, we experience these archetypes when we play these spiritual roles, when we inspire, challenge, and help others on the path to higher states of being, or when others inspire and guide us to do the same. Priests and gurus make a profession of it. Ideal parents and grandparents do it from a sense of love and duty.

The emotional mother figure would be more concerned with getting along with others and being a good citizen, the spiritual mother figure with accomplishing great things. Frank Lloyd Wright's mother, it is reported, put photographs of the world's great architectural achievements on the walls of his nursery and told him he was going to be the greatest architect that ever lived. Picasso's mother told him he would be one of the greatest painters. This is that mother—the guardian of our destiny.

The spiritual father and mother appear negative when their laws are broken and they show their wrath. This is the God in the Old Testament, Caleb's father in *East of Eden*, and fire-and-brimstone preachers. When their charges go stubbornly in the wrong direction and are on the brink of disaster, they withhold their powers, threaten them with hellfire, or kick them out of Paradise.

The spiritual and physical archetypes do not have equal power. The higher, spiritual powers can easily dominate the lower powers if the ego/hero has been initiated and they're in force. We see this in *Dracula*. When the cross (a metaphor of spiritual power) appears, Dracula, despite his incredible physical strength, always shrinks back. Zeus can beat up all the other gods. And in *Raiders of the Lost Ark*, when the spiritual powers locked in the Ark of the Covenant are suddenly unleashed, an evil army of Nazis is dissolved like melting wax.

The Anima/Animus Archetypes

According to Carl Jung, the **anima** is the inner figure of woman held by a man and the **animus** is the inner figure of man at work in the woman's psyche. They are subliminal to consciousness and function from within the unconscious psyche. They benefit but can also endanger consciousness, hence their positive and negative sides. They act as guides to the soul and become necessary links with creative possibilities and instruments of individuation—individuation being Jung's path to a fully realized individual.

In great stories, the positive anima and animus archetypes are expressed as the **positive female** and **male love interests** of the hero. We call the negative anima and animus figures the **temptress** and the **tempter**.

We encounter the positive anima in just about every story that has a male hero. She is the feminine love interest. She helps to lure the hero into the adventure and acts as his guide. She is Beatrice in Dante's *Inferno*, the Indian girl in *Dances with Wolves*, Eva Marie Saint in *On the Waterfront*, Andie MacDowell in *Groundhog Day*, and Gwyneth Paltrow in *Shakespeare In Love*.

Psychologically, she's a man's inner vision of divine beauty and the source of his most productive fantasies. In real life, she's the girl he falls in love with and wants to marry, the girl he makes promises and commitments to. Her love inspires him and is a major source of positive reinforcement. Under her spell, he longs to be a real hero, a man of honor, a man who acts courageously and meets his obligations. And if his character is flawed, she's the one who can shape him up or pressure him to get out there and make it happen.

The negative anima is the temptress, the young witch, the femme fatale. She uses sex to lure the hero and the antihero to their doom. This is Glenn Close in *Fatal Attraction*, Kathleen Turner in *Body Heat*, and Sharon Stone in *Basic Instinct*. Psychologically, she's the inner seductress who hides in the centerfolds of a man's mind and she is a major ally of the great snake. In real life, she is a real fatal attraction.

The positive animus (male love interest) is the ideal husband and lover to the feminine hero. He protects, rescues, and guides. He is her contact to the soul. He is *Amor* to *Psyche*, Superman to Lois Lane, the general's son to Mulan, and Leonardo DiCaprio to Kate Winslet in *Titanic*, the one who guides her away from suicide, a disastrous marriage, and a frigid death.

Patrick Swayze in *Ghost* would be a perfect animus figure, guiding Demi Moore from the other side, if Demi Moore wasn't so passive. As it is, Swayze is both the animus figure and the hero. It is his adventure. If he were a true animus figure (that is, if she were the real hero), it would be a perfect metaphor for this male psychological component which does, in fact, try to influence and guide the feminine ego from the other side of consciousness.

The negative animus (tempter) is the negative male counterpart at work in the woman's psyche. Like the temptress, he is a major ally of the great snake, so he tries to sexually seduce, undermine, and enslave the feminine ego, but he can also be experienced psychologically as a highly critical inner voice. In real life and story, men taken over by this archetype can be real bastards, a brutal husband or lover, or a dictatorial male chauvinist pig. He locks his women in a pumpkin shell, a tower, a kitchen, a psychological or real dungeon. He ridicules her ideas, criticizes her appearance, is insanely jealous, and tries to squash any desires she may have for independence. If she's susceptible to substance abuse, he may help her get hooked. And if they run short of money, he may turn her into a prostitute and even become her pimp.

In a milder, more romantic form, it's Count Varonsky in *Anna*

Karenina. In a less manly, more unpleasant mode, it's the boyfriend in *Tess*. In its most virulent strain, it's *Bluebeard* or Terence Stamp in a movie called *The Collector*. It's the husband of Julia Roberts in *Sleeping with the Enemy* or all the male characters in *Thelma and Louise*.

The Threshold Guardians

When we try to make these journeys, the **threshold guardians** are certain obstacles and barriers that stand in our way. They are there to test our resolve and question our preparedness.

Psychologically, it can be our doubts and our fears—the fear of criticism, rejection, or failure that prevents us from moving forward courageously. In real life, it's the phone call we're afraid to make to ask for a date or a job. Or it's the people who tell us that something we want to do can't be done and if we attempt it, we will fail. But they're there to test our preparedness. When we're ready to do what we really need to do, then we have to push through these barriers.

One of Joseph Campbell's favorite examples is a ferocious demon guardian that stands in front of a Japanese temple. The demon's authoritative right hand is held out in an intimidating gesture that says, "Don't you dare go beyond this point," while its left hand signals from below with a gentler gesture that encourages you to come in, if you are ready. In stories, these guardian qualities manifest themselves as the doorman, henchman, or bureaucrats that try to block the hero's path. Or it's the dragon that guards the treasure or the Doberman pinschers that guard the villain's estate. In fact, it's anyone or anything that tries to discourage, frighten, head off, slow down, or otherwise stop the hero's progress.

One of the best examples in recent times is the subway ghost in the movie *Ghost*. Patrick Swayze has to get downtown to see a psychic helper, but a belligerent, aggressive ghost he runs into on the subway scares him off. In a later attempt, he stands up to the ghost and the ghost is transformed into a helper.

The Trickster

The function of the **trickster** is to stir up trouble and bring about change or progress in any way that it can. The trickster is an essential psychological, fail-safe tool designed to help get us restarted when we're stuck.

Joseph Campbell talks about Edshu, an important trickster character of the Yoruba tribe in West Africa. Edshu walks through a village wearing a hat with four sides and each side is a different color. After he's gone, someone will say, "Hey, did you see that god in the red hat that just walked by?" And someone else will counter, "What do you mean? He was wearing a blue hat." An argument breaks out, the village is polarized, and that brings about important change.

The guy who sold Jack the magic beans is a trickster character and so is Marley's ghost in *A Christmas Carol*. Coyote and Raven are important trickster figures in American Indian mythology.

Joseph Wiseman in *Viva Zapata!* is a negative trickster. He's an anarchist who keeps switching sides and stirring up trouble, first to get a revolution going, then a counterrevolution.

In real life and psychologically, it's anything from slips of the tongue to personal accidents that get us into trouble or concern us so much that we're forced to change. In the real world, a disaster or catastrophe that brings about reforms is a kind of trickster.

CHAPTER 16

SOME SPECIAL QUALITIES
OF METAPHOR

Relativity

The first special quality is relativity. And what this means is that inside the magic circle of a story everything is relative, the same symbol can represent different things in different stories depending on its context. The meaning of a metaphor is determined by its relation to the whole.

If the entity is a kingdom and the prince is in the ego/hero position, the story is about him. His father, the king (or his mother, the queen) would make an excellent metaphor for the higher self. But what if the story is about the king, and he is in the ego/hero position? Then you would have to shop around for something higher, like an emperor or empress, to stand for the higher self and complete the equation. And if the emperor is in the ego/hero position, then you might have to bring in the pope to play the higher role. And if the pope is the hero, then God himself might have to make an appearance. What a symbol represents depends on its position relative to the conscious center (the ego/hero position) and the whole. So it isn't always easy to know what archetype a metaphor represents, if it's out of context.

Another example of relativity is this. Superman can be the hero and Lois Lane the anima love interest, or Lois Lane can be in the ego/hero position with Superman as her animus love interest and guide. It's all relative. Dracula can be the shadow antagonist (negative male physical archetype) to a young girl hero, or he can be the antihero himself on the downside of the wheel. In other words, the same character can play different archetypal roles in different stories.

The same is true in real life and that is what this important pattern reveals. Which archetypal role we are playing (father or mother figure, negative or positive lover, helper, holdfast, hero, or trickster, etc.) is relative to the situation we happen to be in at the moment and who we're dealing with. It depends on the equation. One daughter may see me as a positive father figure, the other daughter as negative. Sometimes my wife might see me as the hero or positive animus figure, but at other times, when I'm being critical, she may experience me as a negative animus figure. I might see her in the morning as a guide to the soul and at night as a temptress. My protégés might see me as a mentor or guide (positive mental father figure), and people who disagree with my politics might see me as a dangerous troublemaker or negative trickster. It's all relative. And it's all revealed in story.

The One and the Many

The next special quality is **the one and the many**. And this means that the major archetypes can be divided into any number of characters. You can have one spiritual God, as in the Old Testament, or hundreds of gods, as did the Hindus and ancient Greeks. You can have one villain and hero or an army of villains and heroes, one goddess of the arts or nine muses. Or these archetypal elements can be combined. The one God in the Old Testament actually represents all of the major archetypes, positive and negative, in one majestic figurehead. Mary Tyler Moore in *Ordinary People* is both the positive and negative mother, and so are Kali, Isis, and Hera. Lee J. Cobb in *On the Waterfront* is both the holdfast and Mr. Big, the evil behind all evils. In *Star Wars* you have separate characters, Darth Vader and the Evil Emperor, playing those two roles. If one character is used, then all the different dimensions are contained in that one metaphor; if hundreds of different characters, then each one represents a different aspect or dimension of the underlying archetype. A house with one room or a palace with a hundred rooms can be a metaphor of the psyche. It all depends on how much detail you want to go into. In *The Longest Day*, a film about the invasion

88

of Normandy Beach in World War II, the whole Allied army is in the ego/hero position. Each different character featured in that invading force represents a different aspect of that archetype. The same is true of *The Iliad*. The whole Greek army is acting as a collective hero. In the movie *The Dirty Dozen*, you have twelve commandos carrying out the same mission. In *Armageddon*, you have a team of ten or more heroes trying to divert the asteroid. Each member of the team represents a different aspect of consciousness. In fairy tales the king often has three sons, all of which are in the ego/hero position. The first two will bungle the king's task and the third will do it right. In *Hansel and Gretel*, you have two different aspects of the ego consciousness (one male, the other female) tackling the same problem.

What all of this reflects is that each of these major psychic dimensions has many separate functions (in psychology they're called complexes) and each of these separate functions can be expressed separately or combined. And then the major archetypes themselves can operate on their own or in concert with the other major players. They are, in fact, very much like the colors of the spectrum. They can be appreciated in their own right, or combined to form white (one God), or separated and mixed together to create a thousand different color combinations.

The Hero's Profession

Because of the divisibility of these archetypes, the hero can have any profession you can name. The specialties of the different professions are all functions of the ego, and each of these special functions can be personified as a different hero. We can easily see these different functions operating psychologically when we're in difficulty. When we're sick, our ego-doctor has to handle it and decide if the illness is serious. Will it cure itself or should we call the doctor? Then after we've been to the doctor, we have to decide whether we trust him and his treatment, and so on. When we're being sued or trying to figure out some mystery, then the ego-lawyer or ego-detective has to step in and handle those problems. In real life, it's the real doctors, lawyers, detectives, and priests who specialize in these different functions and handle these specialized problems. The judge specializes in making judgments, the artist specializes in creating, the detective in detecting. Whatever career you choose, you are specializing in that conscious function. It's what division of labor is all about, different people specializing in different psychic functions.

In a story, we see this revealed by the different professions of the hero, each different profession being a metaphor for that particular conscious function. The detective represents the part of our conscious self that solves mysteries, the investigative reporter the part that seeks out the truth. Some of the other more prevalent contemporary heroes are the cop, the private detective, the superhero crime fighter, the adventurer, the soldier (warrior), the spy, the lawyer, the doctor, the athlete, the archaeologist, the explorer, the teacher, the astronaut, and the judge. Each of these professions or occupations expresses a different function of the conscious self. By far the most popular of these story professions is the crime fighter. And perhaps their popularity stems from the fact that these conscious functions are at the cutting edge of the real world's rather desperate struggle against evil. The society we live in is rife with serious crime—mass murders, serial killings, terrorist bombings; drugs; the kidnapping, rape, abuse, and murder of our children; criminal neglect and corruption on the part of government officials; organized crime; corrupt corporations; corrupt doctors, lawyers, and judges. The crime fighters in our society are at the leading edge of the fight to bring these evils under control, and many of them, unfortunately, are corrupt themselves. In truth, we are in a life-and-death struggle with the dark side of our nature. Psychologically, we are all trying to come to terms with these impulses and tendencies in our own psyches.

The Dominant Trait

What is true of the different conscious functions (or professional specialties) is also true of a person's **dominant trait**, which can also be isolated and personified. Sherlock Holmes is a detective, that's his profession. His dominant quality or trait is deductive reasoning. Othello's dominant trait is jealousy, as is the wicked queen's in *Snow White*. The dominant trait of King Midas is greed. Ebenezer Scrooge's is miserliness. Charlie Chaplin's tramp's is perseverance. Don Juan's is lust. Fred Astaire's dominant trait is charm. Woody Allen's is neurosis or more specifically hypochondria. The dominant trait of Achilles is anger. *The Iliad* is everything you ever wanted to know about anger, its destructive power, and how it can be transferred or resolved. Macbeth shows us the ins and outs of guilt. Sir Lancelot is an icon of chivalry. Jiminy Cricket is Pinocchio's conscience. Jack Nicholson's dominant trait in *Terms of Endearment* and *The Witches of Eastwick* is lechery. All of which are significant revelations of character.

The dominant trait is a factor in real life as well. The mind has many facets and qualities. At different times we're dominated by different traits: anger when we're angry, loyalty when we're loyal, patience when we're being tolerant, and so on. For clarity's sake, story likes to isolate and examine one dimension at a time and show how it operates.

Shapeshifting

The final special quality is **shapeshifting**. Psychologically, shapeshifting means that the powerful, positive and negative archetypal energies of the psyche can take on a variety of forms and attitudes when they interact with consciousness. They can be mild-mannered like Clark Kent or all-powerful like Superman. They can be charming and cordial like Jack Nicholson at the beginning of *The Witches of Eastwick* or ferocious and deadly like the demon he is transformed into at the end. Generally speaking, these powerful unconscious energies hold back their real power and true identities in order to protect consciousness, which is easily frightened and a little slow on the uptake. This is especially true in dreams where they will take a variety of innocuous forms to facilitate communication. All of this is revealed in story. The really heavy-hitter metaphors like Shiva, Krishna, and Zeus rarely, if ever, reveal their true forms to mortals for this very reason. It could endanger or destroy them. In *Oh, God!*, John Denver asked George Burns (God) why he appeared to him as an old man. And George Burns explained that he took that form because it was something that John Denver could easily relate to and not feel threatened by.

On the other hand, our conscious selves, when confronting the outside world, are like wizards and masters of disguise. We have the ability to change our personalities and our personas to suit a variety of situations. We can be vastly different things to different people. This is revealed in story by a character's ability to change form or utilize a disguise. Disguises are a perfect metaphor for the way we change our personas. Which is why audiences take such delight in them.

We can also be psychologically transformed. We can do things that compromise or restore our personalities. This is revealed in story by enchantments or transformations—a prince is turned into a frog or a beast, an old hag is transformed into a princess, a wooden puppet is changed into a real boy.

Also, when we are taken over by an emotion, it changes who we are for the moment, and a character like the Hulk, who changes from an ordinary man into an enormous green bruiser when he's angry, tells us a lot about those transformations.

All of these intriguing metaphors have something important to say about the talents and versatility possessed by the human psyche. Its ability to adjust its character and transform itself into a thousand different operating modes as easily as a chameleon changes color is nothing short of phenomenal. All of the wonders of a great story are, in fact, just easy tricks for the human mind.

CHAPTER 17

GROUP PHENOMENA AND THE ENTITY BEING TRANSFORMED

The reason we experience these archetypes in real life is that the groups human beings form tend to organize themselves much as the psyche does because they are the result of the same fundamental forces. The individual is an expression of the cell, and the tribes, corporations, governments, and all the other groups we form are expressions of the individual. The individual and the group were molded by the same evolutionary forces, so they tend to be analogous—to reflect the same types of organization and psychology, and the same archetypes.

So, if you compare the president of a country or corporation, the chief of a tribe, the captain of a ship, or the governor or king of a state to the ego, you'll discover that they all have the same function in relation to the whole. They are all, like the ego, decision-making, judgment-oriented, task-creating administrators. The ego functions as the governor, the king, the president of our entire being.

Then if you compare the Congress, the board of directors, the elders of the tribe, or the admiralty to the higher self, you'll find that they also have the same function in relation to the whole. They are all policymakers, lawgivers, overseers, and guides. They are really the ones that control the flow of money (energy) and dispense the power. Similarly, if you compare the role of the governed, the workers, the tribespeople, and the ship's crew to the physical body, you'll find that they also have the same relation to the whole. They obey the laws created and administered by the higher bodies and do the work necessary to make the group function.

Then if you add the struggle for power which exists always in every group, and divide the total population or leadership into

93

rival political factions and analyze the objectives of the different factions, an identical model will begin to emerge. You will see in the real world the same struggle between our higher and lower natures to influence and control the seats of power that we see in ourselves and in story. You will see good opposed by evil, criminals opposed by the police, Democrats against Republicans, liberals against conservatives, Fascists against Communists, tyrannies opposed by democracies, and so on. Wherever there are human beings organized in groups, there will be holdfasts overthrowing governments or taking over corporations or unions. And there will be spiritual parent figures trying to reform them, negative emotional parent figures encouraging them, and real heroes opposing them.

And because the human group shares these similarities in organization and function with the human psyche, the human group is an excellent metaphor for the human psyche. You can see this important pattern operating in many great stories and successful films. We call this phenomenon **the entity being transformed.**

In *Star Wars*, the entity being transformed is a galaxy. The galaxy has an archetypal structure (i.e., the forces of good are opposed by the forces of evil and Luke Skywalker is caught in the middle) and it acts as a metaphor of the psyche. And, furthermore, the fate of the galaxy is linked to the destiny of the hero. The ego is part of a greater whole and acts on behalf of the whole psyche, and the fate of the psyche depends on the ego's success. The hero is part of a greater whole and acts on behalf of the whole entity, and the fate of the entity depends on the hero's success. By linking the hero and his or her destiny to the destiny of some group that has this archetypal structure, you create a metaphor of the psyche. And that means a story with extraordinary power.

In James Bond, *Armageddon*, and *Casablanca*, the entity that has this archetypal structure is the world. It acts as a metaphor of the psyche. And the fate of the world is linked to the actions of the hero. In *All the President's Men, King Arthur, Mulan,* and

Braveheart, the entity with an archetypal structure is a country. And the fate of the country is linked to the destiny of the hero. In *Oedipus Rex, Batman, Superman,* and *Mississippi Burning,* the entity with the archetypal structure is a city or a town. And the fate of that entity is linked to the destiny of the hero. In the movie *Hospital*, the entity is a hospital. In *Air Force One*, it's an airplane. In *Titanic*, it's a luxury liner. In *Broadcast News*, it's a network. In *Animal House*, it's a university. In *On the Waterfront*, it's the waterfront. In *Ordinary People*, it's a family. In *Escape from Alcatraz*, it's a prison.

In all of these entities you can identify the archetypal structure—metaphors of higher forces opposed by metaphors of lower forces and the fate of the entity is linked to the destiny of the hero who is caught in the middle. If you study hundreds of great stories and films, you will see this phenomenon at work. It is one of the more important patterns.

CHAPTER 18

THE DYNAMIC CYCLE

Now each of these entities in the real world, whether a country, city, corporation, or individual, is going through the same passages, but at vastly different time scales. The larger the group, the slower their progress. The dynamic that drives these transformations is, as we've indicated, the rivalry between the higher, spiritual forces and the lower, instinctual forces to control the destiny of the entity. The success or failure of the rivals depends on their ability to influence and control the conscious elements that are operating in or near the center (namely, the nascent ego and the holdfast) and to motivate and guide these conscious elements (whether willing or unwilling) through both sides of these consciousness-building passages.

The dynamic works because the higher and lower selves have two very different but complementary agendas. The object of the lower self is to take **possession** of an entity and redirect it toward goals that fulfill its own desires and needs, which are to accumulate, control, and enjoy everything it needs to satisfy its insatiable cravings for sense objects, security, wealth, and territory. In modern terms, we're talking about money, sex, and power. Whenever the opportunity arises, the lower self will try to shut down the influence of the higher self and take control of the entity by capturing the conscious element and transforming it into a holdfast.

Psychologically, it is the appetites and desires of the lower self taking possession of the conscious self and redirecting its goals.

In real life, it's the same thing. Some aspect of the lower self gets control of Saddam Hussein, Lenin, Stalin, Hitler, Ferdinand Marcos, and Idi Amin, and they go after the entity. The tyrant becomes the dictator of the entity, and the negative ego becomes the tyrant of the mind. And when the ego dominates the mind and the tyrant dominates an entity, they attack everything that threatens their dominance and are attracted to anything that can extend their power.

If you wanted to illustrate this phenomenon in story, how would you do that? You would show the villains and the antagonists (the metaphors of the lower self) using the holdfast (the conscious self) to take possession of some entity (the psyche) in order to control its destiny. In *Star Wars*, it's the evil empire taking possession of the galaxy. In *Aliens*, dragon-like monsters take possession of a small planet. In *On the Waterfront*, a mobster has taken control of a union. In *Die Hard*, the villains take over a corporate highrise. In *Under Siege*, it's a warship. In *The Exorcist* and *Dracula*, the Devil and the count take possession of young girls. This idea of evil "taking possession" is a major factor in great stories and another extremely important pattern.

The energies the lower self controls are extremely powerful and seductive, and under the right circumstances, they can easily retake possession of the conscious element. The Devil, as they say, has all the best tunes. When they succeed in this, they pull the conscious element (the holdfast) into their camp, creating the downside of the cycle, and that creates serious problems for the entity as a whole. In our model, we call these serious problems the **states of misfortune**.

In real life, we experience these states of misfortune as the great miseries of the world, as the poverty, crime, pollution, tyranny, famine, injustice, slavery, economic depression, disease, and war that periodically haunt our entity. Psychologically, we experience these negative states as our personal miseries—anxiety, depression, the loss of power, the loss of faith, the loss of self, a poverty of spirit, a sense of hopelessness and despair.

In a story, the state of misfortune is the state of misery (or little bit of hell) that exists within the entity at the beginning of the story. It is the problem of the story that needs to be solved. It can be expressed either as real states of misery and injustice or, in fantasy, as states of enchantment, alien invasions, dragon problems, or exaggerated shark attacks. A bigger-than-life shark attacking an island resort is an excellent way of expressing metaphorically the negative states of being that occur when we are being overwhelmed by negative, unconscious energies. In *Oedipus Rex* the state of misfortune is a plague. In *Exodus*, it's slavery. In *The Iliad*, it's a state of dishonor. In *Armageddon*, it's the threat of death.

The need for higher consciousness springs from the need to resolve these inner and outer states of misfortune. The goal of the higher self is to **liberate** the entity from the tyranny and corruption which caused the state of misfortune and to create a new unified and perfectly balanced whole, a gestalt. As with the holdfast and the lower self, the higher self cannot succeed without the cooperation of a new nascent ego, that is, a new conscious impulse to take the actions necessary to turn things around. The powers controlled by the higher self are also extremely appealing, but even so, the sometimes timid and reluctant nascent ego frequently has to be lured or pushed into the process.

In a story, we see this resolution process as the hero getting involved and solving the problem. In *Star Wars*, Luke Skywalker takes on the evil empire and liberates the galaxy. Sigourney Weaver, in *Aliens*, destroys the terrible mother creature. In *On the Waterfront*, Marlon Brando stands up to the mob and liberates the waterfront. In *Die Hard*, Bruce Willis liberates the hostages. In *The Exorcist* and *Dracula*, a priest and a young man with a wooden stake liberate the young girls. These are perfect metaphors for what we experience psychologically when we have been overcome by a negative unconscious state and then are suddenly liberated.

When the higher self and the ego/hero succeed, however, it creates a new prosperity and a new positive state of being (**state of good fortune**), which in turn creates new opportunities for the lower self to influence and regain control of the ego. This creates a new downside and new problems for the entity, which create the need for more positive actions and new, bigger solutions that require new states of awareness and higher consciousness. This is

98

a continuous cycle all the way up and down the wheel. The old cycle ends with a new state of misfortune. The new cycle begins with another impulse to bring about positive change. With each new state of misfortune, a new and different conscious impulse (or hero) is required. The higher self guides the nascent ego and hero through the upside, then the lower forces guide the transformed holdfast and antihero through the downside. With each pass, the new hero goes up a notch to new levels of exaltation and consciousness.

All of this is revealed in story.

In the *Star Wars* saga, Darth Vader started out as a Jedi, a young hero aligned with the Force, but then he defected to the darkside, became a holdfast, and helped bring about the state of tyranny. Later, with the dawning of a new upside, a new hero, Luke Skywalker, guided by the Force, emerges to oppose him.

In real life, Mikhail Gorbachev starts out as a hero, reforming the Soviet Union. Then he becomes a holdfast, clinging to his power. Boris Yeltsin comes along as the new hero and unseats him. Then Yeltsin becomes another serious holdfast and a new hero has to emerge to undo him. In France, in 1794, a revolution overthrows an unjust monarchy. The well-intentioned revolutionaries regress into Robespierre and the Reign of Terror. Napoleon, the new hero, helps to put an end to that phase but then crowns himself emperor and creates another devastating downside.

In real life, we can also see these cycles very clearly when the solution to one problem helps to create another even more serious problem, which requires another even better solution. For example, a scarcity of food in our early history led to the development of agriculture. That resulted in more food and a sedentary life, and that resulted in the even bigger problem of overpopulation, which we still haven't solved. Nuclear reactors helped solve a major energy problem, then created the even bigger problem of toxic waste. Social security solved the problem of poverty in old age, but that eventually caused enormous deficits.

Balancing the budget helped to lower the deficits, but eventually that could bring on a recession. And on it goes.

These alternating change-of-fortune cycles are the engines that drive this whole process. It's a vicious circle but the net result is higher consciousness. The miracle of our evolution apparently resulted from the need to get out of increasingly more difficult and serious tight spots.

CHAPTER 19

THE HERO'S AND THE ANTIHERO'S JOURNEY

I have divided the passage (one complete cycle of the Golden Paradigm) into eight sections. The four sections on the downside show how the state of misfortune was created and the four sections on the upside show how the state of good fortune is regained. In our story model, I sometimes call this passage the **whole story**, the **backstory**, or the **frame story**. And these are the metaphors that describe the actions and tasks which are necessary to awaken and release the powers that can bring about the change of fortune. Psychologically, it's how consciousness is built up and higher states of being are achieved.

The four sections on the upside of the passage are:
I.   How the Hero Gets Involved in the Passage (or Adventure)
II.   How the Hero Is Initiated
III. How the Hero Is Humbled
IV.   How the Hero Is Rewarded

The four sections on the downside of the passage are:
V.   How the Hero Becomes a Holdfast (and an Antihero)
VI.   How the Antihero Regresses
VII. How the Antihero Becomes a Tyrant
VIII. How the Antihero Is Rewarded

On the downside, evil is aggressive and good is on the defensive. On the upside, it's the reverse—good is aggressive and evil is on the defensive.

Paradise

rebirth

attachment

integration

How the hero
becomes an
antihero

How the hero
is rewarded

How the antihero
regresses

How the hero
is humbled

regression

initiation

How the antihero
becomes a
tyrant

How the hero
is initiated

How the anti-
hero is rewarded

How the hero
gets involved in
the passage

alienation

separation

death

Hell

The downside:
how the state of
misfortunre was
created.

The upside:
how the state of
good fortune
was regained.

To review a whole cycle, we'll use *On the Waterfront,* an important 1950s film starring Marlon Brando. And for argument's sake, we'll pretend that Johnny Friendly, the Lee J. Cobb character, started out as a union hero and only became a holdfast and a criminal later on to keep his power. The story would go something like this:

The young and idealistic Friendly rises up through the ranks (I), opposes and defeats some prior, mildly crooked and dictatorial union boss (II-III), and gets his reward, the union presidency, his bit of paradise (IV). And for awhile everything is jake. He institutes reforms; he is revered by the membership; he loves his job.

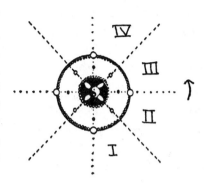

But then it looks like he's not going to be reelected and he doesn't want to give up his power. There's a great deal of inner conflict at first, but gradually the evil influences take hold (V). Negative parent figures become his allies and encourage him in his folly. He suppresses dissent, rifles the pension fund, and takes bribes. He's alienated from the fatherly board and eventually gets rid of them completely (VI). He becomes a tyrant, a new state of misfortune is created, and the union members become serious victims (VII). His compassion is lost; his humanity is lost; all is lost. And he will do anything to keep his power (VIII).

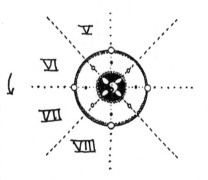

Then a new hero, Marlon Brando, is lured into the process by Eva Marie Saint (positive anima figure) and Karl Malden, a priest (positive spiritual father figure) (I). And Brando goes through a similar initiation and transformation. He brings Johnny Friendly down (II), helps to create a new

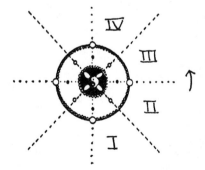

state of good fortune (III), and becomes the new head of the union (IV). Later, when it's his turn to step aside, he too may be reluctant to give up the power and become vulnerable. Then another hero will have to be found to oppose him.

These cycles are a major factor in all of our lives, both psychologically and in the real world. And the plots and metaphors contained in great stories are all about these cycles of possession and liberation, regression and initiation, death and rebirth.

THE DETAILS OF THE PASSAGE*

I. HOW THE HERO GETS INVOLVED IN THE ADVENTURE

At this point in the cycle, a serious **state of misfortune** exists within the entity and action has to be taken. In Joseph Campbell's schema, this is *The Call to Adventure.*

Psychologically, this is the moment when we realize that something is wrong, and the function of the ego which is responsible (the ego-doctor, ego-lawyer, ego-detective, etc.) has to take it on. In real life, Dian Fossey is coming to terms with the plight of the gorillas in Rwanda. Jonas Salk's attention is being focused on the polio virus. Lech Walesa is reacting to the evil actions perpetrated by the Polish government. And Martin Luther King contemplates the horrors being brought about by prejudice and bigotry in the U.S.

In story, the love interest and spiritual father figure enter the hero's world and solicit his help. In *The Verdict*, Jack Warden offers a malpractice case to Paul Newman. In *Armageddon*, Billy Bob Thornton asks Bruce Willis to help stop the asteroid.

Preparedness

Whatever the hero is being called upon to do, it is a potentially dangerous task. We may be ready, like John Wayne or Superman, and willingly take it on as part of our duties. Or we may be reluctant, like Tom Cruise in *The Firm*, and have to be lured or pushed into the process. Or we may refuse altogether, like Willie Loman in *Death of a Salesman*, and have to pay the consequences. In great stories, ninety-nine out of a hundred heroes take up the challenge. In real life, the vast majority refuse. To refuse the call means to let the problems slide and to not become part of the solution. The world remains in trouble and we remain stuck.

* The steps of this passage were built up by information revealed in many stories and shouldn't be confused with the story structure I will describe in Chapter 20, "The Story Focus." Each great story reveals a different aspect of this hidden truth.

If we are **reluctant** to get involved, there are good reasons for it. We have a natural, built-in fear of the forces responsible for these states of misfortune. Correcting the ills of the world or confronting inner demons means opposing the forces responsible for these states of misery. And that can mean putting our conscious elements at considerable risk. Taking on these forces means facing real dangers, real enemies, and very unpleasant truths. These negative forces can make real trouble for us, and we sense that. Unconsciously, we know that behind all of these inner and outer states of misery are forces worth fearing. And this creates a **fear barrier** we are reluctant to cross. We see a good example of this fear in *The Firm*.

A second major problem is that we are severely handicapped. We are in an **inauthentic state**. The society we were brought up in is itself in real trouble, and we are a product of that society. It is going through one of these passages itself and is deep into the downside in an age of alienation and discord, an age of corruption and economic stress in which people have lost touch with their values, each other, and themselves. This is the society we have to conform to, so this is where we get stuck. The inauthentic state is the measure of our stuckness. It is who we are at the beginning of the passage when we're being asked to get involved.

Rick's inauthentic state in *Casablanca* is that he is a disillusioned patriot. Paul Newman in *The Verdict* is an ambulance chaser and an alcoholic. Scrooge is a miser. Pinocchio is a puppet. Pretty woman is a prostitute. The beast in Disney's *Beauty and the Beast* is an enchanted prince, and Will Shakespeare in *Shakespeare In Love* has lost the Muse. Psychologically, these metaphors are incredibly valid, indicating the stultified condition of our conscious selves. Compared to what we could be, we are all like ambulance chasers, drunkards, prostitutes, and people who have lost the Muse. We are all like Robert De Niro in *Awakenings*, Dustin Hoffman in *Rain Man*, and the paralyzed hero in *The Princess Bride*. We are all like little boys and princes that have been turned into puppets, frogs, and beasts or were left "home alone." And going from where we are to where we could be is like going from a puppet to a real boy, or a frog to a prince.

The mind easily accepts all of these inauthentic states as metaphors of our present condition and identifies with them. Then the great stories show us how to become real people again, how to resolve these inauthentic states and become who we were really meant to be. But in order to do that, you have to get involved in the problem and become part of the solution. The clear message of story is: If you want to reach your full potential, then you have to get involved. You have to find your way through the fear barriers and resolve these inauthentic states. You have to identify, oppose, and confront the inner and outer ogres, dragons, and villains that are creating these negative states of being. And you have to overpower, tame, and transform them into something positive. Getting involved in the passage means taking up arms against these inner and outer ills. It means linking your destiny to the fate of an entity that's threatened. It means living and acting like a hero. It means doing what a hero does.

Incentives

But if we are reluctant to get involved because we are full of fear or in an inauthentic state, what is going to get us involved? Obviously, there have to be incentives. The most obvious incentive is the need to save your own skin. In *The Firm*, Tom Cruise is doing it to save his own life and the lives of his family. That's a big incentive. Also, there may be consequences for not acting. If it's technically our responsibility, we can be shamed. Or there can be the promise of positive rewards. In *Star Wars*, the spiritual mentor offers the hero a chance to become a Jedi. No small thing in a galaxy taken over by evil. In *Armageddon*, it's a variety of amusing things plus never having to pay taxes again. Beyond that, it has to fit in with some dream or vision. You have to see it as an opportunity. In *Rain Man*, Tom Cruise sees taking control of his autistic brother as a chance to get rich. Frequently it's the desire to become famous or get the girl. In the beginning it's okay to be motivated, as we all are sometimes, by shallow self-interest because we're in an inauthentic state. Later, we will be transformed into real heroes and those strictly selfish interests will fall away. The journey is a hero-making process.

If the hero is attracted to the love interest, that just makes the love interest's job a lot easier. In real life, as in story, love is the great motivator. The promise of romance is the surest way to lure the hero and ourselves into the adventure.

Linked closely to the incentives are the **fantasies and illusions**. If the desire for the incentives is strong enough and the fear not too extreme, there's a natural tendency to deceive ourselves or be vulnerable to deception. We, or those trying to get us involved, will begin to minimize the difficulties and exaggerate the potential rewards.

When I began the search for the meaning of story, I thought it would take me no more than six months to complete. That was an illusion. And after twenty years on the same journey, I still felt that the next great revelation, which would finally complete the process, was only months away. And that same carrot lured me forward the entire way. That's self-deception.

In an important issue of *Psychology Today*, the cover shows a man wearing rose-colored glasses, and the caption reads: "A Little Self-deception May Be Necessary." And it is. If we knew the real truth up front, we would go the other way. Psychologically, we are being deceived all the time by our unconscious selves. But without this natural tendency, no one would ever put aside practical necessities to pursue knowledge or explore the cosmos.

In a story, we often see this little bit of self-deception expressed as the love interest, the guide to the soul, not telling the hero the whole truth at first. The dangers he will have to face may be too great to reveal (*Chinatown*). When the love interest is not being forthright, this reflects the self-deception necessary to get us involved. And because of its validity, this little bit of deception on the part of the love interest is psychologically very appealing to an audience (*The Maltese Falcon, Shakespeare In Love*), since we are all, in effect, constantly deceiving ourselves.

Commitment

Having been deceived and highly motivated, the hero is ready to make a **commitment**. And this is the item that seals our fate. Once we make a commitment, once we give our word, sign a contract, or take an oath, there's no turning back; we're obligated to deliver. The commitment is the critical factor. Without the commitment, in matters as serious and consequential as these, the follow-through cannot be guaranteed.

When the hero makes a commitment, then the **helpers** appear. This is another of those significant archetypal patterns which reflect an important psychological truth. When we make a definite commitment to ourselves, then the helpers appear, as unexpected insights and ideas or as real helpers in the real world. As long as we're just sitting on the fence, uncommitted and undecided, the helpers don't appear. But the moment we make a definite commitment about something, then the people around us are suddenly full of helpful advice—there's a friend you should talk to, a school you should attend, a book you should read, and so on. The relationship of the helpers to the hero in a story reveals that psychological connection.

Plans and Preparations

After the commitment is made, the hero sketches out a plan and prepares for action. The first objective will be to determine the extent and cause of the problem, who is responsible, and the thing without which the problem cannot be solved (the marvelous element). If some kind of special training is required, then one of the helpers (spiritual, mental, or emotional parent figures) will provide it. In *Star Wars*, Obi-Wan Kenobi has to teach Luke how to use the light saber and how to get in touch with the Force. In *Mulan*, the young girl has to learn how to develop her masculine side as well as be a warrior. In *Armageddon*, Bruce Willis and his crew have to learn how to survive in space. In real life, every passage requires special training. If you're going to be a doctor, a lawyer, a soldier, or an entrepreneur, then you have to have a special education before you take on the problems in those fields.

Self-reliance. The helpers can provide the guidance and instruction we need, the letters of transit, and the amulets to ward off evil, but we have to accomplish the difficult task ourselves. If the helpers do it for us, we will derive very little benefit from the action.

Apprehensions. Other people's lives are affected by the hero's decision. The negative parent figures and negative siblings try to talk us out of it. But we can't be dissuaded. We've made a commitment and our eyes are on the prize. Psychologically, these are the niggling doubts that are always with us but are easy to push aside.

High Hopes and Enthusiasm. The end of this phase is often marked by high hopes and enthusiasm—a genuine conviction that we are going to succeed. In Broadway musicals, it's frequently a big, optimistic musical number at the end of the first act.

II. HOW THE HERO IS INITIATED

The First Reality Is Faced

The hero begins his or her journey. In Joseph Campbell's schema, this is the Road of Trials and Difficult Tasks.

In real life, this is the moment when you take your first step toward the solution to the problem. If you're an investigative reporter, you're out looking for the truth behind the story. If you're Jonas Salk, you're seeking a cure for polio. If you're Lech Walesa, Gandhi, or Martin Luther King, you're taking your revolution into the open. In story, a hero entering an unknown territory or traveling uncharted waters is a perfect way to express what we experience when we enter the world of the problem or probe our unconscious minds seeking a solution.

Problems and Complications. Once involved in the problem, the first thing you will discover is that the situation is much more complicated and difficult than you were led to believe (*The Verdict*). No matter what heroic or non-heroic enterprise or action you undertake, the reality will always be a shock (*The Silence of the Lambs*). The unforeseen and unexpected things that are always out there will invariably make the task more complicated and risky than you supposed (*Armageddon*).

Warnings. The hero's forward motion triggers resistance. And again, no matter what inner or outer state of misfortune you try to reverse, you will be stepping on somebody's toes and you will encounter resistance—which is positive because, if you're doing this part right, you're bringing the complexity and the unconscious cause of the problem to the surface. But the negative energies want nothing to be found out, so they'll do anything to stop you. Usually, however, they won't do more than is necessary to control you or scare you off. If they show more opposition than is necessary, they will give away more of their secrets and that can bring them down. Their first line of defense is a warning. Psychologically, it's the archetypes that give us cautionary feelings. In real life, it's the adversaries who warned Gandhi,

Malcolm X, and Martin Luther King to go no further. These are threshold guardians testing their mettle and their resolve. In a story, the threshold guardian is often a dupe like the police captain in *Dirty Harry* who warns Clint Eastwood to back off.

The hero continues his forward motion and because of his persistence and courage, new helpers appear. If you make the right choices and decisions and take the right actions, you advance, you get more help or information. When we act courageously or do things right, we get assistance. But the more we learn, the more we realize how complex and dangerous things really are.

Temptations. The warnings didn't work so now the villains make their second move. They put the temptress on the hero and offer him a bribe of sex, money, power, or a chance to stay alive. They would still rather own him than kill him.

In real life, the politicians and public officials who have given in to this phase are too numerous to mention. In story, the tempter is an unbelievable sex object or an attaché case filled with money. Satan offered Jesus a chance to rule the world. Hollywood has gotten this one thing right. They know how to personify the seductive inner voices and sensations that are daring us to switch sides and play the other game. If we give in to these temptations, it's the end of the road. We slip back to the downside.

The commitment keeps us moving in a forward direction, but the stakes are being raised and a **second fear barrier** is being created. Unconsciously, we know that all of the negative forces we're opposing are secretly connected. Behind a problem like poverty or prejudice or even a man-eating shark, there may lurk a deadly corruption or neglect (*Jaws*).

Serious Threats. When the hero resists the temptation, the villains get really nasty. When you take on a negative energy in yourself or in others, never underestimate its vehemence or determination to defeat you.

In real life, if you're a politician they may start calling you a Communist or the "L" word and spread vicious rumors about your sexuality. If you're up against the Mafia, they'll send you death threats or put a bomb in your car. If you're Lech Walesa, they may throw you in prison on trumped-up charges. If you were a dissident writer in the old Soviet Union, they put you in a mental institution. This reality is in the background of all of our lives. This is the world we live in, and it's happening every day in every entity. If you are opposing the real villains in our society, whether corrupt politicians or outright criminals, the threats and dangers will be very real. In story, an attempt on the hero's life is the way this step is usually described.

In any case, this is the moment when you realize how serious things really are. The negative energies you're opposing are much more powerful, organized, and deadly than you were led to believe. You were definitely deceived about that. You've put your-self in real jeopardy and an extremely disastrous outcome is highly probable. The second fear barrier is complete and it's much more terrifying than the first. Your heart sinks and your forward motion is temporarily stopped.

The Confrontation

The hero confronts the love interest, the mentor, or the people who have deliberately deceived him (*The Silence of the Lambs*, *Chinatown*, *The Maltese Falcon*). If they don't level with him now, he's going to walk away. Psychologically, this is an inner conflict. You confront your feelings and try to fathom the truth.

When the love interest and the other positive archetypes realize the hero is serious, they show him the victims.

The Victims

The victims are the principal sufferers of the misfortune: the indi-vidual victims of poverty, injustice, bigotry, slavery, tyranny, dis-honor, ignorance, and disease; the victims of the Holocaust, the Apocalypse, the plague; the victims of murder and abuse, crack cocaine, the tobacco industry, and environmentally caused genetic damage. Psychologically, it's that part of our psyches that has been cut off, abducted, murdered, repressed, injured, or abused. We may have been aware of the victims before but our empathy was superficial. Now we are identifying with the real horror of their plight.

When the hero sees the victims, his **compassion** and humanity are awakened. And this brings about a **change of motive** and a **change of character**. Psychologically, this is the moment when we face the full extent of the damage that has been done, and are deeply moved.

If our compassion is not triggered, we will not be transformed. We will remain out of the fight. The passage will end here and the new conscious element will drift to the downside, but not as a holdfast, which is a converted, fully realized hero, but as a negative anima or animus. When the images of children in pain or innocent people suffering starvation leave us cold, then we're not ready for transformation.

In story, this is when Joseph Cotten discovers Orson Welles's bogus penicillin victims in *The Third Man*, Willem Dafoe witnesses a My Lai–type massacre of women and children in *Platoon*, Paul Newman comes face-to-face with the malpractice victim in *The Verdict*, and Jodie Foster sees the mutilated body of a young girl in *The Silence of the Lambs*. Their humanity is jolted awake and they are all transformed. All of these examples are perfect metaphors revealing the forces that bring about this radical change in our feelings.

The hero has proved himself and is told **the truth**. There really is a conspiracy, and powerful and deadly forces like the holdfast are involved. They couldn't tell him the truth before; it would've put all of their lives in jeopardy.

In real life, this is where we learn about death camps, death squads, and secret police, or about corruption and cover-ups and unscrupulous people making obscene profits, or that the tobacco companies not only knew that cigarettes caused death but they processed the nicotine to make them more addictive, and then lied to Congress. Or that J. Edgar Hoover, the man who was supposed to be protecting us, was a vicious blackmailer, a friend to organized crime, and perhaps far worse. Psychologically, if you confront your inner conflicts, shatter an illusion of self-deception and face reality, you will see the truth.

The truth triggers the hero's sense of **outrage**. Our compassion brought about a change of character (*The Verdict*). Now our outrage triggers a sense of duty that overrides personal considerations and fear of consequences (*Platoon*). It gives us the ammunition we need to push through the second fear barrier. It is a major turning point.

In real life, it's the moment when a doctor or lawyer, who has developed a real concern for the interests of his or her patients or clients, is suddenly ready to risk something on their behalf. Or it's the moment when you suddenly become politically active because of your outrage over the environment, the abuse of women and children, or corruption in government. This is also the moment when you realize that as a citizen you have the responsibility to do something about it. In a story, what perfectly describes this experience is the hero becoming ready, despite the threats of personal harm, to risk everything for the sake of the victims (*On the Waterfront, The Verdict, Platoon, The Silence of the Lambs, Mulan*).

Changes of character have to do with resolving our inauthentic states and reconnecting us to others. This reconnection helps to transform us from someone who is self-centered and selfish into a real hero (*Rain Man*). Without this change of character most changes of fortune couldn't occur, since we wouldn't take the risks necessary to complete the task. The key to achieving higher states of consciousness comes from our being able to now do something for others rather than just ourselves. Our motives can be selfish to begin with (it's sometimes necessary to get us involved), but then they change. And ultimately we do something that benefits the world. Without this reconnection, the rest of the passage isn't going to take place. And this is where most of us remain stuck.

The Trap

In Joseph Campbell's schema this is the Supreme Ordeal.

The hero and the love interest devise a brilliant plan and, seeking that without which the problem cannot be solved (the marvelous element), they enter the antagonist's domain. They enter his cave, his castle, his kingdom, or they cross the frontier into his territory. Their presence is detected and something completely unexpected happens. The real force of evil, the dragon or Mr. Big and his enormous power, which they totally underestimated, is suddenly unleashed. It could be Satan (*The Exorcist*), a dozen guys with automatic weapons (*Die Hard*), or a hydra with seven heads (*Hercules*). Their little plan falls apart and they are completely overwhelmed. The love interest is taken prisoner and the hero may be taken prisoner as well. They've accomplished the opposite of what they intended and they're in a terrible fix.

Psychologically, the conscious element will always underestimate the reserve power of the negative unconscious, and when it surfaces antagonistically, it's always a shock and completely disorienting. A twenty-five-foot shark bursting out of the water and smashing a tiny boat is another excellent metaphor for this experience.

In real life, this is a moment when you see the face of evil, when you discover the true extent of the evil and corruption that exists and get a terrifying glimpse of what you're really up against. The negative energy that created Hitler and Stalin really does exist, and you are overwhelmed by it.

For your own protection, this truth about the negative energies and their power, which can be active in yourself and in your adversaries when you face the real world, is carefully and deliberately concealed. If we knew how dangerous these forces really were, before we were prepared to deal with them, we would never venture forth, no matter what the incentives.

The Crisis

The crisis is the second part of the Supreme Ordeal and the final stage of the initiation. It is the turning point, the trigger mechanism and the true middle of the passage. The outcome of this event will determine whether good or bad consequences will follow.

Despair. The hero is in an impossible position. All is apparently lost. The evil power he saw revealed was truly terrifying and undefeatable. He sinks into a black despair.

You will know when you have reached this moment in the real passage when you are facing something you totally fear. Your confidence is shattered, you feel trapped and powerless, you have lost all hope and you fall into a deep despair. The hero tied up in a dungeon or in a deserted warehouse is a perfect way to illustrate this state of mind.

Sacrifice. But the hero cannot dwell on his despair. Our child is in a burning building. Hitler is invading our homeland. A cloud of lethal gas is drifting into our neighborhood. We have to go forward. We have absolutely no choice. If we run away at this stage, we will have a very hard time living with ourselves.

When my children were still young, Diane and I took them to Yosemite National Park for a weekend of camping out. We arrived at ten o'clock at night, and eager for our adventure to begin, we dropped our belongings in the tent we rented and headed into the woods. Fifty yards from the campsite, a huge black bear crashed out of the woods and came charging toward us. My children screamed and ran with their mother back toward the campsite. The bear kept coming and I had no choice but to stand my ground and shine the flashlight I was holding in his charging eyes. He brushed my leg as he ran past me, veered to the left, burst into a picnic area and slapped a garbage can with his paw, which sent it sprawling. Apparently, he wasn't attacking us, but it seemed like a real danger. If I had panicked and left my wife and children unprotected, I couldn't have lived with myself.

So regardless of the risk to ourselves, we can only move in one direction, toward the abominable power, toward our greatest fears. We have to sacrifice ourselves and we have to do it immediately.

But to succeed we need to switch to another brain. We need **superhuman courage** and **strength**. We need instinctual power. The mechanism that triggers this power is our determination to succeed regardless of the cost to ourselves. The moment we make the commitment to sacrifice ourselves, we feel a surge of superhuman power. And that may be accompanied by a revelation or insight that shows us the solution to the problem.

In his book *The Hero with a Thousand Faces*, Joseph Campbell writes:

> "The gods and goddesses [unconscious archetypes] then are to be understood as embodiments and custodians of The Elixir of Imperishable Being [the unmanifest form of the vast potential] but not themselves the Ultimate in its primary state. What the hero seeks through his intercourse with them is therefore not finally themselves, but their grace, i.e., the power of their sustaining substance. This miraculous energy-substance and this alone is the Imperishable; the names and forms of the deities who everywhere embody, dispense, and represent it come and go. This is the miraculous energy of the thunderbolts of Zeus, Yahweh, and the Supreme Buddha, the fertility of the rain of Viracocha, the virtue announced by the bell rung in the mass at the consecration, and the light of the ultimate illumination of the saint and sage. Its guardians dare release it only to the truly proven."

These powerful energies cannot be released willy-nilly. There have to be safeguards and controls, a **trigger mechanism** that is reliable and safe. The commitment to sacrifice is the trigger mechanism which brings about the release of the hero's remarkable powers. You turn on the spiritual power by demonstrating that you have the required strength of character, and that reserve power is given to you.

We were helped through the first fear barrier by fantasies and illusions, through the second by compassion and outrage, and through the third and final fear threshold by a foolproof trap with only one way out—self-sacrifice. We make the commitment, pass the test, and get the thunderbolt. And you can use that power to tame the lower physical forces.

The Final Assault (the Climax)

The Decisive Battle. The hero goes into battle with the principal opponent, and the principal opponent is completely and utterly destroyed. This is the climax of the initiation and the defeat of all of the forces of resistance that opposed the action.

In ancient Greece it was the three hundred Greek warriors that held off the entire Persian army at Thermopylae. In the Crimean War it was the charge of the Light Brigade. In World War I, it was Sergeant York, who single-handedly captured four hundred well-armed German soldiers. In World War II, it was Stalingrad, the extraordinary victories of the RAF over England, and later, the string of Allied victories in Europe from Normandy Beach to the Battle of the Bulge. In the Montreal Olympics it was the U.S. hockey team defeating Russia's world champion professionals. In the 1990s it was Boris Yeltsin and Lech Walesa who helped bring down Gorbachev and the Soviet Union.

In story, it is Daniel Day-Lewis in *The Last of the Mohicans*, Bruce Willis in *Die Hard* taking on a dozen villains one at a time, and Samson killing ten thousand Philistines with the jawbone of an ass. The hero getting or turning on some miraculous power and easily defeating the villain is a perfect metaphor for that function. And the gods releasing a magic sword, an ultimate weapon, or a superhuman strength is a perfect metaphor for that reserve power. And we have seen the hero in this situation a thousand times, achieving an easy victory despite overwhelming odds. Even when it seems implausible we accept it because psychologically, when we are in this mode and the higher powers are vanquishing the lower powers, we are truly undefeatable and invincible. But these powers, as I said, can only be turned on when the ego has been initiated (strengthened). When we regress on the downside, they have to be shut down again. The energies of the spirit cannot be turned over to a faltering ego or antihero who's been taken over by the dark side, without catastrophic and delusional results.

The final obstacle the hero has to overcome is a metaphor of some powerful negative energy that has to be tamed. In *Dracula* it's the sexual desire that onsets in puberty. In *The Iliad* it's anger. In *Snow White* it's jealousy. In James Bond it's power and greed. In *Jaws* and *Jurassic Park*, it's naked aggression. In real life, every uncontrolled release of anger, lust, or aggression is a sign of a crisis which requires a change of attitude to control or transform that negative energy.

When the hero defeats the villain with the help of the higher power, it means that he or she has become master of some aspect of the lower self. The terrible destructive power conjured on the downside has now been transformed and tamed. The hero defeats the villain. The ego subjugates the lower, instinctual energies. Each accomplishment of the ego on the upside tames more and more of this instinctual power.

Assimilation. Having defeated the enemy, the hero strips off his armor or tastes the dragon's blood.

When we face the negative energy that assaults us, we tame and assimilate it. And it empowers us. When you harness or tame these lower powers, you consciously assimilate them and bring them under conscious control. The hero tasting the blood of the dragon he has just slain is a perfect metaphor for our assimilation of these energies. And when Marlon Brando endures the beating of the villains at the end of *On the Waterfront*, he defeats them and gains their power. And that's another excellent way of illustrating this same thing.

III. HOW THE HERO IS HUMBLED

The Marvelous Element. The forces of resistance have been vanquished and the marvelous element which can reverse the state of misfortune is recovered. The synthesis of the newly awakened spiritual power and the assimilation of the lower power creates this new marvelous power—the hidden talent, the ultimate boon, the bright ideas, philosophy, or charisma that could actually positively change the world. These are the miraculous powers we cannot acquire without initiation and they are building blocks of higher consciousness. And in a great story, how would you represent these special energies except as the chalice that possesses Christ consciousness, a crystal that can cure disease, a missing father who can restore wholeness, a lost treasure that can abolish poverty or restore a kingdom, a miraculous fountain that can restore youth, a magic potion that can produce love, a secret weapon or a magic sword that can save the world. These are all excellent metaphors for those potential energies, which are out there, or rather in there somewhere, waiting to be manifest in the right people, at the right time, in the right place.

Sexual Union. The hero and the love interest fall into each other's arms. The hero has done his work well and the guiding feminine soul gives him his reward. This is a moment of ecstasy. It could be something you imagine or something you actually experience during sexual activity. Sex is never better than after some great achievement or success. It is another taste of paradise.

Inflation. The love interest, the power, the heroic deeds, the victory, the lovemaking, the success—it's all too much for the hero and it goes to his head. In real life, you've just had a significant success and you feel elated, bathed in light, significantly above the common sort, or invincible. And you suddenly believe you're the greatest writer, the greatest filmmaker, lawyer, statesman, or soldier that has ever lived. You're a genius, a child of destiny, the true Messiah, the one chosen to save or rule the world.

121

Surge of Power II. The hero acts on the inflation and this triggers another surge of power.

Before it was a dragon or Mr. Big, but this time it is a truly awesome display of unconscious power by the gods which humbles the hero or forces him to flee (magic flight). He barely escapes with his life and has to be rescued (symbolic rebirth).

In World War II spy movies or *Indiana Jones*, after the hero has defeated forty German guards and retrieved the secret formula or lost ark, the awesome power appears as the whole German army and he has to run for his life. In *King Solomon's Mines*, it's an earthquake. In James Bond or *Lethal Weapon* movies, it's the villains' hideout or some building that is about to blow up. In *Pinocchio*, it's the final attack of the whale. In the Hindu myth *Parade of Ants*, it's an ego-shattering reality.

On this point, the message of great stories is very clear: if you act on that inflation, you will be slapped down. You will learn in a very unpleasant way that, despite your success, you are not the world's greatest writer or the new Messiah and you're not invincible. Countless other people have had similar ideas and dreams and a far greater success. Kublai Khan, for instance. But don't fret, you still have an important role to play.

All of this was well known to ancient Chinese sages. In a cosmos filled with heavenly bodies, they reasoned, the role human beings were meant to play can't be very significant. Knowing this has a very sobering and humbling effect. Knowing this, you can accept your fate and, like Indra (*Parade of Ants*), go forward happily playing out the hand you were dealt.

Symbolic Death. The hero is washed up on the beach.

The ego-shattering reality is followed by a depression, which is followed by an acceptance, which leads to a rebirth. With respect to the lower power, the ego has to be strong; with respect to the higher power, the ego has to be humble. First we have to earn the power, then we have to learn how to use it wisely.

In any event, the hero falling overboard in a storm and being rescued or washed up on the beach like Odysseus or Pinocchio in a symbolic death is a perfect metaphor for what we experience when we are brought back down to earth.

IV. HOW THE HERO IS REWARDED

The Return. Now, strengthened on the one hand and humbled on the other, the hero is truly centered. He is reborn. He returns with his boon and the state of misfortune is reversed. In real life, this is when you put your special talents and gifts to work for mankind, when you become a benefit to the world. If you're Jonas Salk, you put your cure for polio on the market. If you're Ted Turner, you give a billion dollars to charity. If you're William Shakespeare you write the world's greatest plays.

In a story, the villains are brought to justice, the galaxy is liberated, or the sheriff of Balboa Island returns with proof that the shark is dead. In *The Verdict*, Paul Newman's victory in court helps mankind by discouraging malpractice. In *The Temple of Doom*, Indiana Jones helps the villagers by returning the sacred crystal and the children. In *The Fiery Waters of Tubertynte*, the hero uses the healing waters to cure the Queen of Erin.

Ascendency. This leads to a rise in the hero's status, to his ascendency. He becomes a knight, a prince, or a king, or he ascends into Heaven and is deified. In real life, our standing is raised because of our courage and accomplishments and we become celebrities, five-star generals, CEOs, and maybe even President. Psychologically, this is the moment when you transcend, when there is an atonement and you become one with some aspect of the self and that aspect is deified. A saint or the son of God rising into Heaven is a perfect metaphor for how that feels.

Mystical Marriage. When you become a boon to mankind and your status is raised (i.e., you have transcended), then the anima or animus comes to you and there is a synthesis, a symbolic marriage, a union of opposites. When you start doing it right, the love interest comes to you. You become irresistible to him or her. This is true in all the realms.

Celebration. There is an incredible celebration. What else would be appropriate?

New Home. Then the hero and his or her spouse occupy their new home, their little bit of paradise. Psychologically, you experience a new, elevated state of mind and feel the joy, the rapture, ecstasy, and bliss you previously only had tastes of. This is the end of the journey, the symbolic returning home. In real life, if you reach this summit, what can I say, you feel great.

THE DOWNSIDE

V. HOW THE HERO BECOMES AN ANTIHERO (HOLDFAST)

VI. HOW THE ANTIHERO REGRESSES

VII. HOW THE ANTIHERO BECOMES A TYRANT

VIII. HOW THE ANTIHERO IS REWARDED

The downside is the exact opposite of the upside. Having achieved a great success, we will—like Adam and Eve, Samson, King David, and Theseus—become vulnerable, an easy target for temptation. The greater our success, the greater our vulnerability. And this is so true it's a cliché. Despite all of their virtues, many of our greatest modern heroes have been transformed into holdfasts and been corrupted or become womanizers.

Having tasted real power, we may be reluctant to give it up. In fact, we may develop an insatiable thirst for more and more power. And that will make us even more vulnerable. Plus there are other problems and pressures that can affect this process. A renewed, general prosperity can lead to decadence as it did in Germany before World War II and in the Roman Empire. Or the threat of outside enemies can put pressure on the entity to concentrate power in its leaders. Then there can be impatience on the part of the new leader with democratic processes or with others in authority. "Why can't these puny minds see the importance of my Napoleonic visions? For the sake of the people I've got to do away with them." And so on. All of this can contribute to our vulnerability.

In any case, we are drawn into the downside and new dark powers will be awakened which will transform the current state of good fortune into new states of misfortune, and a new hero will have to be found to oppose them. The forces of assistance now become the forces of resistance, and the forces of resistance become the forces guiding and aiding the antihero toward his doom. Where there was initiation there is now **regression**; where there was integration there is now **alienation**; where there was strength there is now weakness; where there was love there is now lust; where there was unity there is now polarity; where there was light there is now darkness; where there was a prince there is now a tyrant; where there was a superhero there is now a Wolf Man or a Mr. Hyde; and where the hero's humanity was being awakened, the antihero's humanity is being shut down. His generosity has become uncontrolled greed; his compassion, hatred and loathing. Where there were celebrations there are now orgies; and where there was a paradise there is now a living hell.

The demise of the antihero is more often than not connected to his **overreach,** his uncontrolled greed. Even with $15 billion, Pablo Escobar, Ferdinand Marcos, and Saddam Hussein can't stop themselves. They have to keep accumulating. The misery they create finally becomes unbearable and they have to be destroyed. A new hero with a vision, a new Gandhi or Lech Walesa, takes up the cause and goes after them. And each time around there's a gain. It is three steps forward and two steps back.

In story, Adam and Eve, Samson, King David, Theseus, Oedipus, *Medea, Faust, Othello, Macbeth, Dr. Jekyll and Mr. Hyde, Little Caesar, The Grapes of Wrath, The Wolf Man, Gone with the Wind, Snow White, Citizen Kane, Body Heat, Basic Instinct,* the downside of *Raging Bull,* and *The Godfather,* to name just a few, help to outline and illuminate this path.

Psychologically, what this means is that we grow in stages. Consciousness is built up bit by bit by this process. Nascent egos are continually being born. They mature and regress. They become old egos reluctant to step aside and have to be deposed by strong new impulses to change. If the old holdfast ego is too strong and the new nascent ego too weak (and the helpers are not in place), then we get stuck, which is what is happening to most people today.

CHAPTER 20

THE STORY FOCUS

We encounter this same passage or cycle, as I said, in every entity and in all the major passages of our lives. We are, in fact, experiencing many of these cycles at once as we simultaneously seek wealth, wisdom, love, health, freedom, justice, and other important values for ourselves, our families, our clients, our country, or the world.

Every problem we face and every action we take is related to one or another of these cycles. And in the course of a single day, we may experience dozens of these different cycles. We may be on the upside of some of these passages, the downside of others; the initiation stage of one cycle and the regression stage of another; the problem and complication phase of one and the crisis phase of another; the reluctance, climax, or inflation stage of yet another. We may be heroic in some passages, and holdfasts or completely stuck in others. Our ego-doctor could be handling one problem successfully, but our ego-lawyer is getting us into serious legal trouble. Our business can be doing well while our love life is a catastrophe. Then our love life improves and our company goes belly up. Our health is on the upside but our house is being destroyed by an earthquake or a flood. Crime is down in our neighborhood but our country is going to war. Each of these events belongs to a different cycle.

We are also involved in the cycles of other people in which we are playing a variety of archetypal roles. We participate in the cycles of our children, as parental forces of assistance and resistance, when they are experiencing the tyranny of the terrible twos and other periodic downsides. We participate in the cycles of our friends and family members, as threshold guardians and guides, when they're getting hooked on alcohol, cigarettes, or drugs, and when they're being liberated from these substances. In fact, everyone we are involved with is managing the same cluster of cycles and we are participating in them on all different levels, playing many different roles. We are also participating in the up-and-down cycles of our communities, our cities, our nations and states. And in this respect we carry a profile similar to that of the President, the conscious, decision-making center of the country, who has to deal with a multiplicity of personal problems and cycles while simultaneously waging war on the nation's poverty, injustice, bigotry, ignorance, terrorism, crime, and disease. Each of which is part of a different cycle. And all of which we may somehow be involved in. Each time we recycle a bit of plastic or pick litter up off the street, we are participating in, and having an effect on, the larger war on pollution, which is part of a very serious downside and being fought worldwide. Every political action we take, in fact, including just casting a vote for a candidate who has promised to act like a hero, is a participation in one of these cycles.

We can manage all this because our extraordinary brains can divide the dozen or so whole cycles we're experiencing simultaneously into a sequence of smaller, manageable events or problems, block out what might distract us, and focus on one thing at a time. Then we can shift our attention from one cycle to another and solve one of these smaller problems as necessity dictates. One problem solved or partly solved, we then switch back to some other new or partly solved problem in one of the other cycles.

We don't notice that each of these individual problems is part of a structured cycle because we are experiencing the different cycles in a seemingly random fashion and are constantly shifting our attention from one cycle to another, which makes us think we're experiencing a completely random shift of thoughts and moods. But we aren't. We're experiencing an extraordinary and complex web of interrelated cycles and passages which are governed by the pursuit of some important value like wealth, health, freedom, or justice, and by the avoidance of their opposites— poverty, disease, slavery, and injustice.

All of this is revealed in story, which for clarity's sake, likes to isolate one of these value cycles, focus on one aspect, and examine it in great detail.

The Trojan War

In *The Iliad,* for instance, the aspect of the whole passage being explored in detail has to do with anger. Achilles and Agamemnon have an argument over a girl who was given to Achilles as a prize. Agamemnon takes the girl back—Achilles feels dishonored, gets angry, and drops out of the fight. The Greek army falls apart without him and is almost destroyed. The story ends when Achilles lets go of his anger and returns to the fight. But this incident, which encompasses the entire book of *The Iliad*, is only a very small part of the *whole story.**

This *whole story*, which reveals the passage, has to do with the wrath of two goddesses, Hera and Athena, who despise Paris because, in a contest to determine the fairest goddess, he chose Aphrodite over them. They are so put out, they plot the downfall of Paris and Troy. And after Aphrodite rewards Paris by helping him to seduce Helen (the downside), the offended goddesses help her husband, King Menelaus, raise the army he needs to attack Troy and get her back (the upside). They're nine years into the war when the tragic incident between Agamemnon and Achilles occurs, and the *whole story* is revealed through that one extremely narrow focus. The episode involving the Trojan horse, which is the real climax of the passage, doesn't occur until a year after *The Iliad* ends, and isn't even mentioned in that story.

The way the *whole story* and the story focus are structured and related to each other is the metaphor that illustrates with great clarity how the mind isolates one cycle and focuses on one aspect.

The Odyssey is another focus on that same *whole story* and reveals other details of the passage. It begins a long time after the

* In our story model, we call the passages of the Golden Paradigm the whole story, and the smaller story—i.e., that aspect of the whole story which is being focused on—the story focus

129

fall of Troy and is all about the ten-year struggle of Odysseus to return home. You could create a hundred other stories, each focusing on a different aspect of that one passage. And that is, in fact, what Euripides and a large number of other Greek dramatists did (*Iphigenia, The Trojan Women, Orestes,* etc.)

The Iliad—The Whole Story

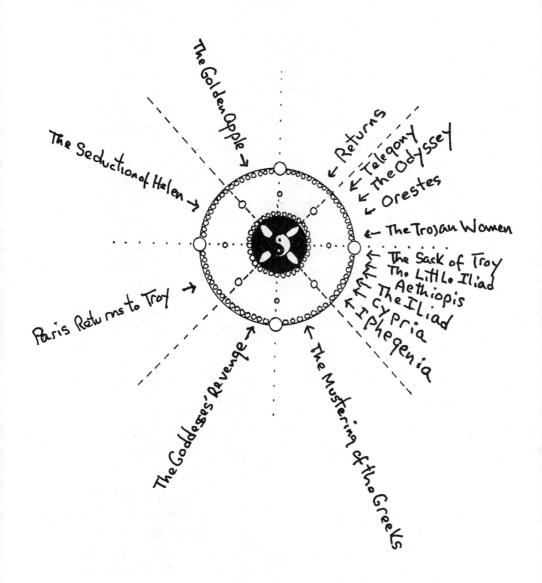

The value being pursued in the *whole story* of *The Iliad* is honor (and the avoidance of its opposite, dishonor) and every facet of the *whole story* is an exploration of that subject. The goddesses feel dishonored when Paris selects Aphrodite. Menelaus feels dishonored when Paris seduces his wife, Helen. Achilles feels dishonored when Agamemnon takes away his prize. Poseidon feels dishonored when Odysseus destroys his statue during the sack of Troy. Each individual story (or *story focus*) reveals a different aspect of that hidden truth. No single story could begin to reveal everything contained in the passage, which is far too vast and complex and technically has no end. Most stories created today are about lawlessness and are focused on the upside in sections I and II. They begin with the hero getting involved in an adventure and end with a climactic battle with the villain. And this could reflect our preoccupation with the problems of inauthenticity and crime—and the serious need we have to gain control over our negative energies.

World War II

Using World War II as another *whole story* which reveals the passage, you can see a similar example in modern times. Hitler takes over Europe (the downside) and the Allies band together to destroy him and liberate the continent (the upside). The value being pursued is freedom, the scourge being avoided is tyranny and the slavery that implies. *The Longest Day*, a focus on that *whole story*, is all about D-Day, the taking of Normandy Beach by the Allied forces. Like *The Iliad* the entire story is focused on that one battle, but the *whole story*, World War II, is very much in the background.

In *Saving Private Ryan*, Spielberg isolates a dilemma of justice and humanity surrounding one individual soldier who is caught up in that same invasion. In *Schindler's List*, another story in the larger context of that same war, hundreds of Jews are rescued from the Holocaust by one enterprising German businessman. In *The Great Escape*, we see a spectacular escape of Allied soldiers from a German prison camp. The entire story is focused on this one event which took place sometime during the crisis phase of the whole passage between the time when the Allied forces invaded Europe and the climax of the *whole story*, the Battle of the Bulge. In *Patton*, the character of the general who engineered this string of victories is thoroughly explored. In *Casablanca*, a former patriot and freedom fighter named Rick has become disillusioned and, like Achilles, dropped out of the fight. The principal action of the story focuses on how Rick is brought back into the fight. And, here again, World War II and the larger questions of tyranny and freedom are ever present in the background.

World War II—The Whole Story

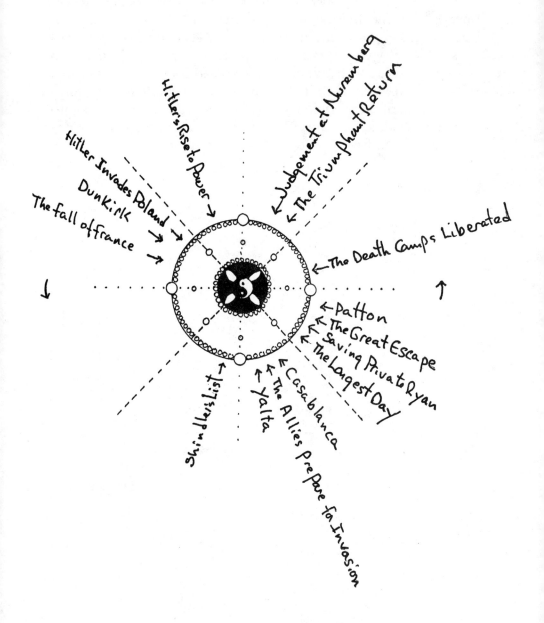

The real war, which started in 1939, ended in 1945 with the occupation of Berlin. The Allied victory was the result of the coordinated efforts of millions of people, all of which were essential to a positive outcome. There is no way you can assess or organize and study all of those details, which are extremely complex and very hard to analyze and draw concrete lessons from. So we need the story to help us understand this event. By dividing the war into stories, you isolate essentials that make it possible for us to see inside this complex web of interrelated events and examine the structures and dimensions we can't ordinarily see because of the confusion of details. Each of the stories mentioned above reveals a different facet of the *whole story* passage of World War II, and that larger story is always referenced. And that is how the mind looks at big events and fathoms their complexity. And when you artistically treat these stories, you ferret out a hidden truth that can tell us a lot about our own psychology and the real causes of the war. All of which make story a very useful tool.

King Arthur

The myriad legends of King Arthur sketch out three complete *whole story* cycles. The first upside cycle begins with Arthur's father, King Uther Pendragon, unifying the country. On the downside of the first cycle, Pendragon is taken over by lust and the unification falls apart. The second upside cycle involves the young King Arthur who, with the help of Merlin and the miraculous sword,

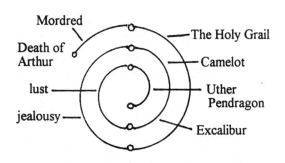

Excalibur, reunifies the country and creates Camelot. This renewed state of good fortune then falls completely apart because of jealousy, creating another downside. The only thing that can

save the kingdom after that is the Holy Grail and that sparks the upside of a third cycle, wherein Sir Galahad and the other most virtuous knights pursue the quest for the Holy Grail. This is eventually achieved, but then the whole thing falls apart again with the rise of Mordred, the evil, illegitimate son of Arthur, who ultimately brings about his father's death.

Each different adventure of all of the different knights illuminates some other dimension of the whole, and if you take the time to analyze all of the stories associated with all of these cycles, you will see how they overlap, how one story takes up where another leaves off, and so on. If you do this with enough stories and piece them together, the much larger, coherent structure of the passage will be revealed. And that is how the structures of the Golden Paradigm and storywheel were discovered. If you build your story model using only the things that all stories have in common, you will miss the structure created by their differences.

Types of Story Focus

In real life, when we are involved in one of these cycles and some action has to be taken, the types of things we focus on are similar to those outlined in the first four stages of the passage, and consequently, there are four types of critical action that a story will focus on.

The first type takes place in section I of the passage and is focused on the character of the hero and has to do with getting the hero to join or return to the fight. In these stories, the hero is in an inauthentic state. He (or she) has gotten off the track and is not dealing with the problem, and the story is focusing on him and his problem rather than some other important action. These heroes are either enchanted (*Beauty and the Beast, Pinocchio*), on the wrong side (*On the Waterfront, A Christmas Carol*), reluctant to get involved (*Alexander Nevsky, High Noon*), or they have lost something (*Shakespeare In Love*), or have dropped out of the fight entirely (*The Iliad, Casablanca*). These stories are about the transformation of the hero's character and show the hero being brought back to a heroic frame of mind and returning to the fight. The *whole story*, of course, is always referenced in the background.

In this type of story on the downside of the passage, the story is focused on the corruption rather than the rehabilitation of some antihero. *Othello, Macbeth, Body Heat, Basic Instinct, The Godfather*, and *Faust* are all focused on the downside. John Milton's *Paradise Lost* begins after the *whole story*'s great battle between God and Satan and is all about Satan's efforts to corrupt Adam and Eve. *Macbeth*, which begins on the upside after the climactic battle, is focused on the downside and is all about Macbeth's corruption and guilt. *Othello* is focused on jealousy and is all about the destruction of the Moor by his servant, Iago. In all of these cases, the larger, *whole story* is always in the background.

A second type of story is focused in the initiation stage (II). The hero has been brought into the fight and the focus shifts toward the major and minor direct actions the hero has to perform—i.e., the battles that have to be fought to liberate the entity (*Star Wars, Jaws, The Longest Day*), or the power that has to be gained to win those battles (*The Holy Grail, Excalibur*). In stories of direct action, the hero's character is not in question. He is in an authentic, heroic state. He realizes his place in the scheme, accepts his responsibility, takes action, and accepts his fate. He is in the fight and on track, discovering, pursuing, and defeating the cause of the problem and evolving to a higher state of consciousness. The story is focused around some decisive action and illustrates how that is done. It could be the main action of the initiation (*Star Wars*) or a single battle, as in *The Longest Day*.

A third type of story is focused on the events that take place in sections III and IV, after the conclusion of the initiation. Those in section III focus on the hero's inflation or on his encounter and escape from the final surge of negative power. The return of Odysseus in *The Odyssey* is one example, the Hindu myth *Parade of Ants*, another. *Parade* begins after the climax of the *whole story*'s great battle, which is alluded to in the exposition,

137

and is all about the inflation and humbling of the god Indra. Those in section IV focus on the resolution of the problem, the transcendence of the hero, the wedding or the celebration, and they give us a glimpse of paradise. In *Father of the Bride*, the entire story focuses on a single incident, the wedding, and the *whole story* is revealed in the context of that one event. In *My Dinner with André*, the entire two-hour film covers a single dinner conversation between two men. This remarkable and very entertaining film, which takes place somewhere in IV after the hero's return, works because one of the participants acts as a storyteller and reveals the *whole story* through his personal adventure from disillusioned artist to reborn spiritual man.

These very important patterns make us aware of the types of situations we will encounter in the passage and the things we will need to focus on.

The Structures and Dynamics of the Story Focus

Wherever we are focused on the wheel, we not only have to be aware of the problem and the solution of the focus, we have to know how our actions relate to the big picture and how they will affect the future. The structure of the story focus illuminates this:

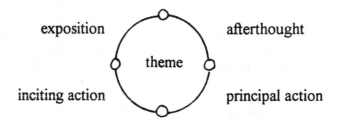

The thematic element—the anger, inflation, etc., that is being focused on—is in the center. In developing the focus, we explore the relation of that thematic element to the value of the *whole story*. In *Casablanca*, the subject of the *whole story* on the

138

downside is tyranny. The value being pursued on the upside is freedom. The theme of the focus is patriotism. The story reveals how patriotism relates to tyranny and freedom: i.e., you can't defeat tyranny and regain freedom without it.

The **inciting action** is the downside action that describes the problem of the focus, and the **principal action** is an upside action which shows us how this particular problem is resolved. The two subordinate structures of the focus are the **exposition** and the **afterthought**. They relate the focus to the whole passage. The exposition links it to past and present events and the afterthought links it to the future. This structure is a perfect illustration of how our minds are functioning when we're focusing on a problem that's related to one of these passages.

The *whole story* behind *Casablanca*, as we mentioned, is World War II, and the focus of that *whole story* is the transformation of one individual, an ex-patriot named Rick who has dropped out of the fight. But the *whole story* is always very much in the background. That comes to us from the exposition. The inciting action tells us how Rick became disillusioned in Paris and lost his patriotism, and the principal action shows us how Rick gets that patriotism back. The afterthought is everything we know is going to happen after Rick and Claude Rains disappear into the fog: i.e. we know that Rick is now back in the fight and will play an important role in the war.

The Principal Action

The most important of these structures is the principal action because that is the action that solves the problem and brings about the change of fortune. In real life, a problem-solving, principal action is interrupted by problems from other cycles and it's hard to know where one experience begins and another ends. In story, these principal actions and their components are separated from all the other cycles, artistically treated, and reconstructed into an unbroken unity that can be studied when we're motivated to look beyond the sugar coat at what's hidden inside.

In real life, after we've analyzed the problem, we create a **theory** and a **plan** which will continually be adjusted until the problem is solved. The principal action is the main objective of that plan. It is the central, unifying action that leads to the defeat of Hitler, the tracking down of a serial killer, or the victory over some injustice. In a great story, it's these things plus the actions necessary to solve a dragon or alien problem. In *The Exorcist*, it's casting out the Devil. In *Raiders of the Lost Ark*, it's finding the lost ark. In *Parade of Ants*, it's the actions that lead to the humbling of Indra.

This central action holds these stories together and gives them a **unity of action**. According to Aristotle, "The imitation [of a story] is one when the object imitated is one. So the plot, being an imitation of an action, must imitate one action, and the whole of that [one action]."

The principal action in story is also, as in life, the line of action that causes all of the antagonism and resistance and is the source of the greatest tension and suspense. The real key to understanding story and problem-solving actions in real life is the understanding of the structures hidden in this principal action.

In real life, this principal action is also the action that brings about the change of fortune.

To quote Aristotle again: "The proper magnitude [of a story] is comprised within such limits that the sequence of events, according to the laws of probability and necessity, will admit of a change from bad fortune to good or from good fortune to bad."

In *The Exorcist*, the little girl is possessed by the Devil. The principal action, casting out the Devil, brings about a state of good fortune. On the downside, it's the reverse. In *Othello*, a state of good fortune exists at the beginning. The principal action, perpetrated by Iago, destroys the Moor with jealousy and a state of tragic misfortune is the result.

Great stories are all about changes of fortune and the principal actions that bring them about. In real life, every action we take as heroes brings about a change of fortune. It is an extremely important pattern, and they are two of the most important and useful things a storymaker can know about story and a human being can know about life.

The Structures of the Principal Action

The principal action has four structures: the solution formula, the genre structure, the universal structure, and the classical structure.

The Solution Formula

In real life, we automatically divide the principal action into a number of other important actions which are necessary to carry out our plan and bring about the solution. These larger actions can in turn be divided into other, even smaller subordinate actions, and the right combination of these smaller actions will create a **solution formula.**

In a story, the methods the heroes use to solve their problems reveal these solution formulas, and in a great story, these actions can, and should, actually teach us how to catch a serial killer, solve a shark problem, transform a miser, unseat a tyrant, and so on. And the more elegant the solution, the more hidden truth it contains.

The Genre Structure

The second structure of the principal action is the **genre structure.**

The actions of the solution formula are made up of mental, emotional, physical, and spiritual elements. Every problem-solving action we take will have these four dimensions working in concert. One of those elements will be dominant, and that dominant element will give the problem its emotional, mental, physical, or spiritual character, and the other dimensions will be subordinate. If the problem we are trying to solve is physical, then emotional and mental factors have to be involved if the main problem is to be resolved. If the problems are emotional, then mental and

141

physical factors have to be worked out as well, and so on. In other words, to perform one of these necessary actions you need the coordinated efforts of the *mind*, the *body*, the *heart*, and the *soul*. You can't solve a problem of one of these dimensions without the involvement of the other dimensions.

In story, the **plots** and **subplots** of the principal action are derived from these organic structures and reveal how the heart, mind, body, and soul work together to accomplish the actions of the solution. We call stories and actions dominated by the mental aspect *mysteries*, those dominated by the emotional aspect *love stories*, those dominated by the physical aspect *war stories*, and those dominated by the spiritual aspect *transcendental stories*.

In *Jaws* and in *Rocky*, the **dominant plot** (principal action) is physical (a war with a shark and a prizefighter's war with his own body), but the emotional and mental elements, which are subordinate, also have to be worked out in order to succeed. In *Jaws*, Roy Scheider has to work out relationships with the contradictory experts and solve mysteries concerning the shark's intentions, its habits, size, strengths, and weaknesses. In *Rocky*, to succeed as a fighter, Sylvester Stallone has to work out relationships with Talia Shire and her brother, and solve the mystery of his own fears (*Rocky*) and the loss of his courage (*Rocky II* and *III*).

In *Sherlock Holmes*, the dominant plot is mental (a mystery) and the emotional (love story) and physical (war story) are subplots. In other words, the dominant element is a mystery: Who did it? The main tension is released when the mystery is solved, when the killer is identified. Very often the physical adventure (war story) is nothing more than a tussle over the gun the killer has pulled after being identified.

In *Casablanca*, the dominant plot is a love story. The most important thread that has to be worked out is Rick's relationship with Ilsa. He has to understand why she didn't show up at the railway station in Paris. The mystery surrounding Rick's neutrality, the transcendental powers of the letters of transit, and the physical struggle with the Germans and the Vichy government are minor by comparison. This is why it is thought of as a love story.

The Universal Structure

The third structure is the **universal structure**. Sometimes when you carry out one of these problem-solving actions, you will get the desired result. Other times you will not and you will need the universal structure to complete the task. This universal structure is an essential unit of action that can be described by the formula: $T + E + R + P = DR$. **Trial** plus **error** plus **reflection** plus **perseverance** equals **desired result**. We take an action (trial), and the result is different than we anticipated (error). There is, as Robert McKee describes it, a gap between expectation and result. We reassess the result, adjust our theory, revise our plan (reflection), and take another action. And we keep doing this until the problem is solved (perseverance).

You will find this process in everything you do—from trying to find the right screw in a jar filled with different-sized screws to landing a man on the moon. You try something and if that doesn't work, you try something else. There is almost no other way to solve a problem.

All of this is revealed in story. In *Groundhog Day*, to get out of his rut, Bill Murray has to repeat this universal action hundreds of times until he finally gets it right. Usually, the hero only has to do it two or three times. The climactic actions of *Alien* and *Terminator* are other good examples of this very important pattern.

The Classical Structure

More often than not this trial-and-error process will lead you through the phases of the final and most important structure of action, the **classical structure**. Its basic components are: **complications, reversal, crisis, discovery, climax,** and **resolution,** all of which were outlined in the initiation phase of the passage.

143

Armed with our theory, our plan and the trial-and-error process, we set out to accomplish a task and encounter a series of **complications**. These complications frequently lead to a **reversal** (i.e., the opposite of what we intended). The reversal leads to a **crisis** (the apparent defeat of our best efforts), and the crisis leads to a **discovery** (an insight that can lead to a solution). All of this leads to the climactic actions necessary to bring about a solution (**climax**), and the climax leads to a **resolution** (a transformation back to a state of good fortune).

This classical structure is critical because this is the structure that brings the negative energies to the surface and sets them up for transformation. No matter what problem-solving action we undertake, we will encounter and need these components. This too is revealed in story.

In *Jaws*, a shark starts eating tourists at the height of the season (state of misfortune). The sheriff, Roy Scheider, and two shark experts set out to track it down (principal action). Their boat, it turns out, isn't big enough and one of the shark experts is off his rocker (complications). The shark gets the upper hand and smashes their boat (reversal) and their boat is sinking (crisis). As the disaster progresses, Scheider realizes the shark will swallow anything, including a tank of explosive gas (discovery). He jams the tank into the shark's mouth, shoots it, and blows the shark to oblivion (climax). The shark dead, peace and prosperity are restored to Balboa Island (resolution). The state of misfortune has been changed back to a state of good fortune.

You will see this structure in important minor actions in real life and story, as well. If the hero is breaking into the villain's office, he may have trouble picking the lock (complications), then the night watchman is heard coming (crisis), he realizes he's been using the wrong tool (discovery), he finds the right tool and opens the door (climax) and gets safely inside (resolution). Our lives, in fact, are defined by these elements. Whether we're trying to hunt and gather, build a pyramid, defeat Hitler, discover a unified field theory, create a story, put on a wedding, or repair a damaged relationship, we will encounter this structure.

The Essence of Story

This *Classical Structure* (along with the principal action, inciting incident, and change of fortune) has been a major factor in human affairs and in stories created in the oral tradition for tens, if not hundreds, of thousands of years. It has been a major factor in stories written by individual authors since Aristotle first described it 2,400 years ago. The early Greek dramatists who evolved this dramatic structure, which Aristotle observed, had tapped into these dimensions of real life—the principles of dramatic action being, in fact, the laws of action in real life artistically treated. This is important to know because it relates *Classical Structure* to the structure of action in real life.

Now I will describe the connection between *Classical Structure* and the **essence of story** (that without which there would be no story). And here again we will find these very same elements. Without a principal action to guide the viewer's attention and a change of fortune, there is no story. If the story ends in the same place it began without some significant progress up or down, the audience will wonder what the point of it was. It will be a very unsatisfactory experience. Without complications and a crisis, there is no story. If Cinderella goes to the ball, falls in love with the prince and marries him without a single hitch, or if Indiana Jones goes after the Holy Grail and finds it without running into any difficulty whatsoever, there is no story. The audience is left muttering, "So what?" And if there's a crisis but no climax and no resolution, you will have the same problem. You will leave your audience feeling completely unfulfilled. They will have the distinct feeling that the story was left unfinished.

This is important stuff because it links *Classical Structure* not only to the structures of action in real life but to the very essence of story—that without which there would be no story. And if it involves the essence of story, it must be very important indeed.

Stories, after all, hide the secrets of life, so the essence of story must, of necessity, hide one of its deepest secrets. And so it does. It is in fact the action that took the human mind up the evolutionary path. Pursuing happiness, health, wealth, freedom, and justice, we encountered resistance, we confronted problems and sought solutions. We tried this and we tried that. The unforeseen created the complications, and persistence provoked the negative energies and triggered an unexpected response. We thought it over, revised our theories and our plans, took another action, and passed through the classical structure. And this ordeal gave us the information we needed to solve the problem and reach a resolution. This is how problems were solved then, and this is how problems are solved now. That is how the negative energies of the lower self are brought into the open and transformed, and this is how consciousness is built up bit by bit. It is the key to the passage, the key to higher consciousness, the key to everything.

Storywise, however, there are still some vital ingredients missing. A story can have a principal action with a classical structure and still not make any sense, if it's out of context with some larger whole. If you rely on classical structure as your understanding of story, you're in serious trouble. You can struggle with that model all of your life and still not have a story come out right. In real life, if you are pursuing these actions without knowing they are connected to a greater whole, they will come to nothing.

That is why Joseph Campbell's work is so important. His monomyth, The Hero's Journey, connects story to the real purpose of story and gives significance to the types of actions which need to be selected. It also begins to reveal the transcendental structures that can guide the hero and ourselves to higher states of being.

The Golden Paradigm then takes things a step further and demonstrates why Classical Structure and The Hero's Journey need to be connected to the larger, **whole story passage** if it is to have real power and meaning. Only then do we see clearly that the real structures of a great story are a mirror of the human mind in transformation.

Wisdom

Every action in real life contains a lesson and this is how we learn. We depend on these lessons to build our experience. Each time you take an action and get an unexpected or disappointing result, you learn something. Each time you take an action and discover the cause of a problem, you learn something. If the lesson is strong enough, then the incident is worth repeating, and you can retell it like a story and share that lesson.

In great stories, the lesson is revealed by the main bit of wisdom the action contains. Each great story acts out an important general truth that can be applied to many different situations. The actions of the story demonstrate that wisdom. It is the lesson of the action. If the bit of wisdom conveyed by the story is that crime doesn't pay, then the action of the story will act that out. The criminal will come to some terrible end and we will come to that conclusion.

In *Casablanca*, the wisdom is: When it comes to matters of the heart, don't make assumptions; things are never what they seem. When Ilsa didn't show up at the railroad station in Paris, Rick assumed it meant she had lied to him about her feelings. And if that love was false, it makes everything else, including the war, pointless. He becomes disillusioned and drops out of the fight. Later, he discovers the truth. She had a good reason for not showing up. His assumptions were incorrect. That being resolved, he gets back into the fight.

The wisdom of *The Iliad*, according to Ben Jonson, is: "United we stand, divided we fall." This is clearly demonstrated by the action, which is a treatise on the devastating effects of anger. After the argument with Agamemnon, the angry Achilles and his army drop out of the fight and the Greeks are overrun and ravaged by the Trojans. Later, when unity is restored, Achilles gets back into the fight and the tide changes in favor of the Greeks.

In *Jurassic Park*, the action is clearly advising us to think twice before playing God.

In a great story, the wisdom is never obvious. It is hidden for later discovery. If the wisdom in a story is too obvious, it becomes a moral tale or, worse yet, a story with a message, which is something for the intellect and not the heart.

The Scene

The most important **unit of action** in a story is the **scene**. In real life, certain actions and ideas are more essential to a solution than others. In story, we see this revealed by the structure of the scenes, which isolate the essential steps (the **core elements**) and illuminate them. The core element becomes the center or fascination of the scene. It is what the scene is about. It links the scene to the passage and story focus and governs the actions around which the scene is built. And in a great story the scene will often only have this one objective. And when this is true, then everything in that scene—the actions, the characters, the atmosphere, the mood, the setting, etc., can serve that one objective and create a powerful **artistic statement**.

In Zeffirelli's *Romeo and Juliet*, the balcony scene is all about one thing: the declaration of love. And everything in that scene— the setting, the mood, the music—supports that one idea. And besides helping to make it artistically powerful, limiting the scene to one objective greatly increases the clarity and helps to focus the feelings of the audience. They sink right into the essential feeling. In Dickens's *A Christmas Carol*, the whole beginning has only one objective: to establish that Ebenezer Scrooge is a miser. We see this in the setting and the mood but also in the action. Scrooge is counting his money. Cratchit is cold but is allowed to use only one piece of coal. Good Samaritans arrive trying to raise funds for the poor and Scrooge turns them away. *The Godfather* (Part I) has sixty or so short filmic scenes which are made potent by their simplicity. In *Snow White* there are fourteen or so fully illuminated and enriched scenes making up the whole film, which

148

is why these films are so effective. The simpler the scenes, the richer they are: the clearer their meaning, and the stronger their impact emotionally.

CHAPTER 21

THE SUGAR COAT

The sugar coat refers to the **entertainment dimensions**, which are the pleasant sensations the audience feels when they experience your story. In real life, they are the jumble of feelings we experience as we jump from cycle to cycle. In a great story, they are one set of these feelings isolated and purified so they can be experienced together in a meaningful sequence. They are produced by the same metaphors and actions that reveal the hidden truth and are strengthened by the intensity of that hidden truth. The promise of these feelings helps to lure the audience into the experience, and the fulfillment of that promise gives them pleasure and a sense of having been entertained. And the closer you get to the hidden truth, the more powerful the feelings. The more powerful the feelings, the more our interest is heightened and our excitement aroused.

These entertainment dimensions are created by isolation. When you isolate a story element, you focus attention on that element and heighten the interest and emotional involvement. And when you artistically treat that story element, you purify and intensify the hidden truth it contains. That purified, intensified truth is highly charged with the emotional values we experience as entertainment.

The most important of these feelings are those associated with the actions of the genre structures that we discussed in the previous chapter. When you isolate the plots and subplots of these genre structures, you separate the threads and create actions and scenes that are directly linked to specific feelings associated with romance, mystery, adventure, or some other particular activity. Besides **laughter** and **tears** there are four other major dimensions—**passion, suspense, excitement, magic**—and numerous minor dimensions—**love, hate, fear, terror, awe, horror, hope,** despair, desire, disgust, enchantment, sympathy, attraction, lust, anger and surprise. These are the feelings the audience experiences when the hero guides them through the paradigm. These feelings are like flags that mark the way, and the sequence of these feelings will help the audience identify the experience when they're ready to make a meaningful connection. They only need to ask themselves what caused those feelings and they will begin to see the hidden patterns.

A great story, of course, excites all of these different feelings, which are associated with the progressive steps of the passage. Every great story will have a moment of terror, for instance. But in a horror movie like *Scream 2*, the filmmakers isolate the actions and situations that produce terror and keep repeating them, giving the audience stronger and stronger doses of this same emotion. It is a compliment to the power of this one dimension that it has produced so many successes in this one genre, but imagine the power of a story that has all these entertainment dimensions, fully realized.

In any case, the emotional values that make up the sugar coat are enhanced by a number of factors. The first is **make-believe**. Make-believe separates the intriguing aspects and mechanics of a given situation from the fear of the consequences we might experience in real life. In real life, nothing could be less entertaining or enlightening than a real serial killer stalking your neighborhood. Your only concern would be to get rid of him as soon as possible. In a story, where you can eliminate the fear of consequences, you are left with the pleasant sensations associated with the hunt, and you can study the mechanics of that experience objectively. Using this separation, a story can artistically treat and translate even the most horrible real crimes into an intriguing entertainment that conceals an important truth in a powerful metaphor.

Another factor is **structure**. Separated from the fear of consequences, the archetypal rivalry which can be so deadly in real life becomes a game in story. The same structures, in fact, that make a game fun make a story fun—i.e., the fact that it involves oppos-ing sides, important things at stake, a marvelous element, possi-ble victories or defeats, and a ticking clock. The only difference between an ordinary game like football and the story game is the size of the playing field, which in story can be as big as a galaxy (*Star Wars*). And that is to say, as big as the human mind.

Another factor augmenting the sugar coat is **real life**. Audiences are fascinated and delighted by successful imitations of real life—real human gestures, expressions, moods, and conversation. When a great story artistically treats real life to create a metaphor, it retains that fascination and becomes a primary interest holder. It rivets their attention.

Two final factors are the technical and aesthetic dimensions. The **aesthetic dimensions—clarity, beauty, elegance, harmony, rhythm, grace**, etc.—are the pleasing effects that are created by the skillful and artistic use of the **technical dimensions—variety, contrast, proportion, symmetry, timing, tempo**, etc. Proportion and symmetry are major factors in the creation of beauty. And perfect proportion, like beauty itself, is a noble torment of the mind. Contrast is a major factor in creating clarity. When you contrast such things as good and evil, spiritual and physical, rich and poor, light and dark, silence and sounds, you heighten the effect of both and greatly increase the clarity. Rhythm is the key to elegance and grace. Perfect rhythm is the ideal combination of repetition and variety (similarity and change). A story has a cer-tain rhythm. Every different type of story has a different rhythm. This is true of tempo and pace as well. Real life has its own spe-cial tempo and pace, and every different type of story (mystery, love story, action adventure, etc.) has its own characteristic tempo and pace. *Das Boot*, *The Lifeguard*, and *The Culpepper Cattle Company* are worth studying in this regard. Their pace seems synchronized with some internal, organic tempo and pace.

All of the hundred or so powerful metaphors and dimensions that create a great story have an impact on the sugar coat, on the entertainment values of the story, and the more dimensions (truth) the story contains, the greater the emotional impact on the audience. The good news here being that great stories not only contain the secrets of life, these hidden secrets make them superpowerful and extremely entertaining. And those two ingredients—power and entertainment—are the keys to a great success.

CHAPTER 22

THE STORYWHEEL

Like the passages of the Golden Paradigm, the storywheel has an upside and a downside and is divided into eight sections.

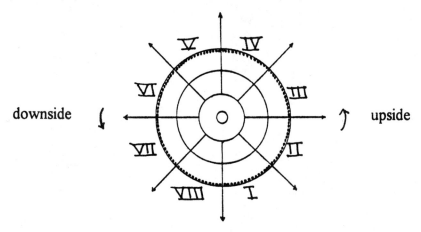

The four sections on the upside reveal the passages from birth to zenith; the four sections on the downside, the passages from zenith to nadir (or death). Stories that end on the downside have unhappy or tragic endings. The antihero gives in to temptation and slips down the ladder to a lower plane. Stories that end on the upside have happy endings. The hero resists temptation and goes up the ladder to a higher plane.

The stories in section I help relate individuals to themselves or their family, or otherwise prepare them for life. I call these stories **fairy tales**, but they also include all other stories of childhood and youth. The stories in section II help relate the individual to society. They show us how to resolve an inauthentic state, how to establish our careers, how to raise a family, how to love, and so on. I call these stories **classics**. The stories in section III relate the individual to the world at large. The heroes in this category sacrifice themselves for people they don't even know. They show us how to release our superhuman powers, how to become a great professional, or how to cope with inflation if we become a great success. I call these stories **legends**. The stories in section IV relate the individual to the cosmos, to God, or the spiritual dimension. In these stories the heroes transcend. They reach their full potential. I call these stories **myths**. The stories in section V show us how the individual is alienated from the cosmos, from God, or the spiritual dimension. I call these stories **anti-myths**. The **anti-legends** in section VI show us how the individual is alienated from the world at large. In section VII we see the **anti-classics** and learn how the individual is alienated from his or her society. Among these are **anti-love stories**, like *Othello*, which show us how lovers are alienated from each other rather than brought together. In the final section, VIII, we see **anti-fairy tales** and learn about the alienation of the individual from his or her self.

The Storywheel

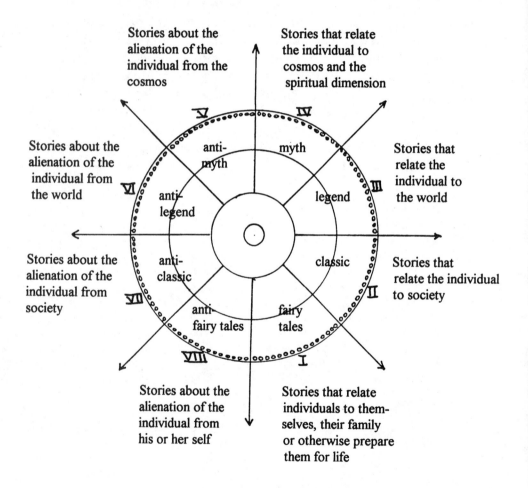

Zenith

Stories about the alienation of the individual from the cosmos

Stories that relate the individual to cosmos and the spiritual dimension

Stories about the alienation of the individual from the world

Stories that relate the individual to the world

Stories about the alienation of the individual from society

Stories that relate the individual to society

Stories about the alienation of the individual from his or her self

Stories that relate individuals to themselves, their family or otherwise prepare them for life

anti-myth   myth

anti-legend   legend

anti-classic   classic

anti fairy tales   fairy tales

V   IV   III   II   I   VIII   VII   VI

Nadir

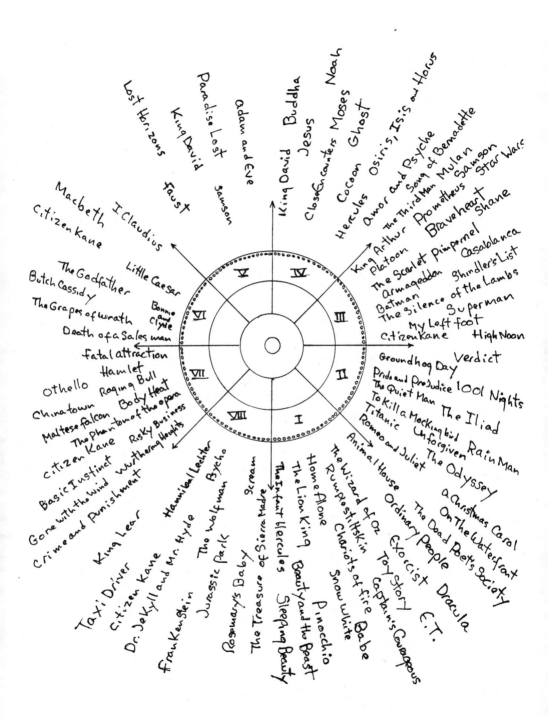

The Source of Wisdom and Power

When I was seven years old, I wanted to be Captain Marvel, a superhero like Superman. In everyday life, Marvel was a crippled newsboy named Billy Batson. But when he needed to become Captain Marvel to fight evil or protect the innocent, he cried out "Shazam!" and was hit by a lightning bolt, and that lightning bolt transformed him into the superhero.

On Thanksgiving of that year, when my whole family gathered at my Aunt Marie's for our traditional Thanksgiving dinner, I snuck into one of the empty bedrooms and spent three hours alone in that room praying to God to make me Captain Marvel. And with tears in my eyes and all the sincerity I could muster (at that age it was my dominant trait), I promised to use the power only to do good.

After three hours, I stood before the mirror on the dresser, trembling with a sense of destiny, and having absolutely no doubt that I was about to be transformed into the most powerful force for good on earth, I cried out "Shazam," and braced myself for the megavolts. But nothing happened. I repeated the gist of my vows, clenched my fist, and shouted the magic word two more times. Still it was in vain. I was stunned and very disappointed. It severely damaged my relations with the Supreme Being.

Thirty years later I realized that the storywheel is Shazam. The great story is Shazam. That is how we transform ourselves from crippled, inauthentic newsboys into human marvels, by following that path. The great story uses its imagery to stimulate our imaginations and give us little tastes of paradise which trigger fantasies that lead us to desires for positive actions in the real world. Then, as we pursue these goals, the stories guide us through the passages using meaningful connections, each story revealing a little bit more of the truth. And piece by piece, bit by bit, drop by drop, the whole truth is gradually revealed. And despite ourselves, we find our selves, realize our dreams, and like Captain Marvel, Hercules, and Psyche, we reach our full potential. The creative unconscious self is the source of that wisdom and that power. The great stories are the guardians of that wisdom and that power. And if you unravel their mysteries and fathom their secrets, you can participate in your own creation.

PART FOUR

THE ART OF STORYMAKING

The poet's eye, in a fine frenzy rolling,
Doth glance from heaven to earth, from earth to heaven;
And, as imagination bodies forth
The forms of things unknown, the poet's pen
Turns them to shapes, and gives to airy nothing
A local habitation and a name.
                    —Shakespeare, *A Midsummer Night's Dream*

CHAPTER 23

THE CREATIVE PROCESS AND THE NEW ARTIST-STORYMAKER

To create something means to bring something forth, to bring something into being, to fashion or produce something that didn't previously exist. In this case a story. Earlier I talked about the natural storymaking process in which the creative unconscious self used the oral tradition to transform an incident worth repeating into a story that contained the secrets of life. This process was cut off, in part because of the written word, leaving billions of people without this vital, life-giving information. The new artist-storymaker perceives this need and has a desire to fulfill it. Armed with a fluency in the language of metaphor and a sophisticated story model, we insert ourselves into this process. We enter into a partnership with the creative unconscious self and use the creative process to construct great stories that will benefit and entertain those who experience them.

The key to all of this is our **feelings**. Feelings are at the threshold between the two worlds and are without a doubt a communication from our unconscious to our conscious self. This link is obvious with physical or spiritual feelings: When we feel physical pain we know something is physically wrong, that it's a communication. And when we experience strong spiritual feelings, we sense they are a message or reward of some kind. But it's less obvious with feelings associated with mental or emotional creative processes. When you play with your creative ideas, the positive and negative feelings you experience are important messages from your creative unconscious self. If you learn how to read these feelings, then playing with your creative ideas becomes a direct means of contact. Every experience of feelings is an attempt to bring unconscious content and influence to consciousness. Getting in touch with your feelings is getting in touch with your self. Getting in touch with your self through your feelings is the heart and soul of the creative process.

Your principal resources are your *imagination*, your *technique*, your *knowledge*, and your *experience*.

Your *imagination* is the image-making function, the process that transforms the raw energy into visual images, into metaphors. It is your ability to create new images and ideas by combining previous experiences. The stored memories of real things are the raw clay. The curious tendencies of the mind are the artistic tools that help to recombine and shape that raw clay into new creative ideas. The process functions freely and automatically and is largely unconscious.

Technique is the conscious function, the method of working which helps you achieve the desired result. The imagination brings the raw material to the surface, and the conscious technique helps to fashion that raw material into a powerful metaphor that contains the hidden truth.

The *knowledge* is the special understanding you possess of your art. It's what you know about story. It's what you need to know to become a master storymaker. The special knowledge I teach in this book has to do with the nature and purpose of story, the language of metaphor, the Golden Paradigm, and the creative process. Without this or some other special knowledge as a point of reference, even a vivid imagination and a great technique won't help you very much.

As for *experience*, there's just no substitute for it. The more you work with these processes, the better you get.

CHAPTER 24

IMITATIONS OF REAL LIFE

What the metaphor is to hidden truth, imitations of real life are to art. This is the artistic dimension that holds the mirror up to nature. And if you aspire to real greatness, this is the dimension you should be most interested in. The writers who master this dimension win Pulitzer and Nobel prizes, the filmmakers who master it win Academy Awards. It defines great acting.

If the artist-storymaker sets out not just to entertain but to explore life and discover truth, you can feel it in their work. It makes a powerful impression. And I'm not just talking about the works of Shakespeare, Dickens, Milton, and Dostoyevsky, I'm talking about motion pictures like *Babette's Feast*, *The Godfather*, *Schindler's List*, *Ordinary People*, *Witness*, and *Raging Bull*. From the very first instant, you realize you're dealing with something of substance. And it doesn't compromise the entertainment, it enhances and intensifies it. A story that is exploring life has a certain very appealing pace and feel to it that draws the audience in and rivets their attention. And you can really see the power of this dimension if you realize that this one quality transformed films like *Fatal Attraction*, *The Exorcist*, and *The Silence of the Lambs* from being simple horror movies into highly acclaimed, realistic dramas—and it added a hundred million dollars to their grosses.

Another virtue of this dimension is camouflage. You should be so embroiled in the lives of the characters that you don't notice the structure, and one of the best ways to do that is to put everything in the context of everyday, real life. In the opening scene of *The Godfather*, Part I, for instance, the main sensation you have is that you're at a wedding, but there are some very heavy plot elements hidden in that context. In another part of the film, on his way to execute a family traitor, one of the hitmen stops at a deli to pick up some sausages for his wife. In another scene, the Corleone family is planning a gang war while making spaghetti together.

Mastery of this dimension is achieved by the observation of life, by observing how people really behave, how they relate to each other—how parents relate to their children, how husbands relate to their wives, and how people really talk. And if you're not a practiced observer, and haven't consciously been observing them, you'll find that people act very differently than you thought. When you live life, you have a subjective point of view. When you observe life, you detach yourself and acquire an objective point of view, and then the experience of life is very different.

Tom Wolfe believes, "The author should be out in the field the same as the reporter, living, observing, and experiencing life."

This is the storymaker's fieldwork. It is also the actor's fieldwork. Meryl Streep said that the thing she regretted most about being a celebrity was that she could no longer ride the subway watching how people behave.

To become a good observer, you have to learn how to see. If you've ever tried to draw a human face or hand, you know what I mean. It's very difficult. An artist has to learn how to see. So does a storymaker.

When I was still in my early twenties, my wife and I were driving around the outskirts of the UCLA campus. We were with our two daughters and happened to be talking about koala bears. Diane said they only eat the leaves of eucalyptus trees, and she pointed to some examples that we just happened to be passing by. I was amazed and asked her how she knew they were eucalyptus trees. (I grew up in New York City and didn't know a tree from a telephone pole.) She laughed at my ignorance and explained how easy it was: you simply looked at the shape of their leaves. Hmm.

I began doing that and became fascinated by trees. I took some botany courses at UCLA and, in my spare time, began walking around the campus or in the Santa Monica Mountains collecting leaf samples and studying their differences. It took awhile but I finally caught on.

My very favorite discovery was a ginkgo tree on the UCLA campus. The ginkgo tree comes from China and has a leaf shaped like this.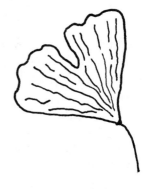

It has been around for over three hundred thousand years and is the most ancient tree species in the world. Its ancientness and the fact that it came from China gave it a mystical quality like a venerable Chinese sage, and I formed a special bond with that tree. For years I was drawn to it. I loved to sit under it and contemplate the story model, my own problems, or the fate of the world.

Then one Spring I returned to New York City and was strolling along the streets of my old neighborhood. Much to my surprise I discovered that the streets where I grew up were lined with ginkgo trees. They were everywhere and had been there since before I was born. I had played with my soldiers under their boughs and never noticed them. It's amazing how much you overlook until you become a practiced observer.

CHAPTER 25

SOURCES OF MATERIAL

To begin with, you can do your own version of an already **existing myth, legend or classic,** and take it the next evolutionary step, in an otherwise cut-off evolutionary process. The biggest names in literature—Homer, Milton, Sophocles, Shakespeare, and Goethe, among others—all did exactly that. They took an existing legend or myth and put their personal stamp on it. If you do that, ninety percent of the work has been done for you by the oral tradition. *The Mists of Avalon* is Marion Zimmer Bradley's version of King Arthur from Morgan le Fay's point of view. *The Seven-Per-Cent Solution* is Nicholas Meyer's take on Sherlock Holmes. *Mary Reilly* is a maid's-eye view of *Dr. Jekyll and Mr. Hyde. Beauty and the Beast* is how Disney sees that classic, and so on.

A second possibility has to do with taking a **real incident worth repeating** and creating either a true or fictional story out of that event by finding the archetypes and the model in the true story and artistically treating the subject. *JFK* is Oliver Stone's retelling of the Kennedy assassination. *In Cold Blood* is Truman Capote's re-creation of the brutal murder of a midwestern family. *All the President's Men* is an artistic treatment of the events surrounding the Watergate burglary.

A third way to start would be to analyze the old great stories and discover the **precedent structures,** which are the underlying motifs, and redress them in an entirely new costume. If you analyze *Alien,* you will find *Beowulf.* Grendel taking possession of a castle and devouring its knights one by one, and an alien monster taking over a spaceship and devouring its crew one by one, are similar metaphors with similar meanings being made relevant by differences of time and place. If you analyze *The Lion King,* you will find *Hamlet.* An evil uncle murders his brother, steals his kingdom and queen, and tries to prevent his nephew, the rightful heir, from assuming the throne. The change of time and place, and a change from human to animal, do not affect the meaning of the metaphor. They just make it more accessible to children.

If you analyze *Groundhog Day*, you will find *Beauty and the Beast*. To break his enchantment, a "beast" has to learn how to love and be worthy of love. If you analyze *On the Waterfront*, you will find *Mutiny on the Bounty*. A basically ethical henchman, on the wrong side, is transformed by love and can no longer tolerate injustice. If you analyze *West Side Story* and *Pretty Woman*, you will find *Romeo and Juliet* and *Cinderella*. And so on. These precedent structures are adaptable to any age or time.

A final option is to evolve a completely original idea, starting with a fascination, which is what I will show you how to do in chapter 27.

CHAPTER 26

SIX CREATIVE TECHNIQUES

Whichever path you choose, the creative process and the creative tools will be the same. You will use the true or imagined material as your starting place (as your fascination) and follow the same creative steps. The creative process I am describing utilizes six **creative techniques**. The first is called "probing the fascination."

Probing the Fascination

By **fascination** I mean any idea or visual image that has strong feelings attached to it. It could be anything that gets your juices going and inspires you to create a story. It could be a piece of music, a favorite song, a fantasy, a dream, some intriguing character or situation, a scene in your head, a haunting memory, a beautiful face, an incredible atmosphere, and so on.

By **probing the fascination** I mean working with that fascination creatively. You experience it, explore it, romance it. You plug it into your imagination in ways that create other images and ideas, the same as you do when you elaborate or give details and structure to a fantasy or daydream. You translate feelings into visual images (into metaphors) and use your imagination to bring more raw, unconscious, story-relevant material to the surface.

The important thing is to engage your feelings because that puts you in touch with your creative unconscious self and the energy behind those images. And when you're in touch with your feelings, you're in touch with your self. You use the fascination as a point of contact with your self, and you translate your feelings into visual images (into metaphors).

Comparing and Selecting

When you probe a fascination, you will generate much more raw material than you need, so the second creative technique involves **comparing and selecting**. You weigh the virtues of one idea against the other, keep the ideas that have the strongest positive feelings attached to them and throw away the rest. Get rid of everything you can and continue to work with the few most powerful ideas. The artistic tools operating here are the tendencies to remember what makes a strong impression and to forget what leaves you cold. Using that as a guide, keep the ideas that haunt you and get rid of the rest. In other words, respect the ideas that have power. The stronger the feelings associated with an idea, the more hidden truth it contains.

Modeling

In the third technique, **modeling,** you examine the emotionally charged images you've selected and begin identifying and associating them with the archetypes of the story model. You listen to the feelings associated with these images and realize that this is the holdfast, this is the state of misfortune, this is the hero, these are the people who lure the hero into the adventure, this is the marvelous element, this event is part of the crisis, and so on.

The model helps to facilitate communication with your creative unconscious self because it was created by the patterns put into great stories by the creative unconscious. And when you use the model as a reference, you create metaphors that make a psychological connection and a syntax that reveals the hidden truth. All of which will be confirmed by your feelings.

Conjuring

In the fourth creative technique, you take the emerging metaphors and evolve them into more and more powerful examples of the archetypes. This is called **conjuring.** When you conjure, you are playing with the developing characters, powers, and events and trying them in a hundred different combinations, like Edison inventing his lightbulb. He tried one hundred and twenty-seven different filaments before he found the right one, tungsten. Here again you are listening to your feelings and trying to discover the most pleasing patterns and potent combinations.

171

You are rearranging things, trying to evolve them into more and more powerful metaphors.

Testing

After you've worked up the whole model, then you **test** the model by walking through it to see how it feels. You walk through the steps of the passage you've sketched out or the scenes of the focus, just to get a sense of how it feels. You take it a beat at a time, being as sensitive as you can to your own response. If something doesn't feel right, then you work on that problem. You take it apart and try something else. You change the characters, shift scenes around, etc. You replace some of the first ideas and walk through it again.

Problem Solving

Face all the problems and negative feelings directly. If something is wrong, take it apart and try something else. Storymaking is mostly confronting and **solving problems**. The more problems and negative feelings you confront and resolve, the better your work is going to be. Any problems left unsolved at the end of the day you can sleep on. Let *Rumplestiltskin* take over and transform your pile of straw into gold while you sleep. More often than not, the problems will be resolved when you wake up in the morning.

Rollo May, who wrote a book called *The Courage to Create*, describes it this way: "You go through a period of intensive work, confront all the dilemmas, conflicts, and blocks, then put it aside and let the unconscious do its work."

Throughout this process, as we've mentioned, you are working with your feelings. Your feelings are helping you make all of the necessary decisions. Everything you do creatively, every change, every thought, every new selection, has a feeling connotation. It will either feel good or bad and you will make your decisions accordingly.

The most important feelings to pay attention to are your negative feelings. These are the unpleasant feelings that you have to learn to tolerate and understand. These are the feelings that can guide you to greatness. Negative feelings counterbalance positive feelings. If we didn't have negative feelings we would be easily satisfied with what we have done, so we wouldn't change it and it would stop growing.

Listening to your feelings is not about being right or wrong or your work being good or bad, it's about being closer to, or farther away from, the truth. It's like the child's game where you're trying to find something and you're being told that you're getting warm or getting cold. Positive feelings mean you're getting warm (closer to the truth), and negative feelings mean you're getting cold (farther away). Listening to your feelings means being guided to the truth by your self. If it doesn't feel right, it isn't right. Something is wrong. You've got a problem. And you resolve that problem by the trial-and-error process; you try different things until the feelings change. Ninety-nine percent of the time negative feelings simply mean that it needs more work or it has to be placed differently or it's almost right but not quite or it really doesn't work. If it really doesn't work, throw out what you have and start over.

You've heard that the artist suffers. This is apparently what that is all about. Artists voluntarily confront and deal with their negative feelings in order to create something and grow. It is a controlled, voluntary suffering for the sake of getting at the truth. Sometimes the feelings and the suffering can get pretty rough. There's usually at least one stage in the process where it gets so desperate and unpleasant you lose all hope and are ready to quit.

Some years ago, when I was preparing this material for a series of seminars I teach, I experienced one of these unpleasant episodes. And during that time I had this dream. I was standing in the doorway of my kitchen just outside the threshold and looking inside. My wife, a notorious anima figure in my dreams, was standing just inside the doorway to the right, facing one of the kitchen counters. Another extremely beautiful but younger girl with dark hair was standing in front of the stove to my left looking directly into my eyes. Just as this was happening, my wife began to melt (like the witch in *The Wizard of Oz*) until all that remained was a puddle of what looked like the vanilla ice cream I ate the night before and one beautiful leg.

I looked back at the beautiful girl in front of the stove. Her look intensified and became challenging, and with her right hand she gestured that I should come to her. Uneasy about doing as she commanded, I stayed outside the doorway. Then I woke up.

I was anxious about the dream and confused by it. Then I suddenly remembered something I had said the day before while preparing the course. When I had reached the place where I say, "And sometimes these feelings get pretty rough . . ." I was considering saying, "If you can't stand the heat, stay out of the kitchen." And then I understood the dream. In terms of negative feelings (heat), I had reached a crisis point in the work. My usual anima and guide was melting away from the new heat being generated by the emerging anima figure who was standing near the stove. This new anima figure was beckoning me to come closer so I could experience this new heat, but I was staying out of the kitchen. In other words, I was being hypocritical. I was about to tell my students that it gets rough and if you can't stand the heat stay out of the kitchen—and the dream was telling me that's exactly what I was doing. There were thresholds of creative suffering I was not ready to take. I was staying out of the kitchen myself.

It took a long time but I finally began working with the "new heat" and I came through it. If you go through it, you come through it. Learn to trust the negative feelings. Negative feelings are, of course, not really negative, but they are unpleasant. Become sensitive also to the subtle micro-feelings like, the princess in *The Princess and the Pea*. Work with them, sail into them, and find out what they're saying. In any event, don't take them personally as a judgment on your work.

CHAPTER 27

CREATING THE MODEL

Several years ago I was sitting in an Italian deli called Gianfranco on Santa Monica Boulevard in Los Angeles. There was music playing in the background. It was one of the choruses from Verdi's opera *Nabucco*, which is about the Jewish slave revolt in Babylon. When it was first performed in Italy over a century ago, it began a civil war. The audience was so moved by the music that they rushed out of the theater and took up arms.

I was hearing this incredible music for the first time. It was during the breakup of the Soviet Union, during the upheavals in Eastern Europe when Communist government after Communist government was being overthrown. It was also the time of the Tiananmen Square student massacre in China.

The particular chorus I was hearing was called "La Pensera" and for me it was the moment of empowerment, the moment when the people feel a surge of power and are ready to risk death for the sake of freedom. I immediately began to weave that fascination into a story about a real revolution that overthrows a corrupt, tyrannical regime and how that revolution came about. I thought about the revolutionary scenes in the movie *Reds* and wanted to make it something real and powerful like that.

When you find something that fascinates you like that, then that becomes your inspiration, your starting point. You plug it into your imagination and work with that fascination until you've created a bounty of other intriguing ideas and fascinations that can also be probed. Ultimately, every character, action, and scene will have its own fascination at its center. Then you select the strongest images and ideas and begin modeling. Everything you need to construct the model can be found in that fascination. And probing that fascination for your other ideas will create a "feel" that gives a unity to the story in the same way that a musical key gives unity to a musical composition.

The archetypal elements which are necessary to construct the model, and which you will discover in that fascination, are: **the value being pursued, the entity being transformed, the state of misfortune, the cause of the problem, the holdfast, the solution to the problem, the marvelous element, the hero, the forces of assistance and resistance** (character archetypes), **conflict,** and **the steps of the passage.**

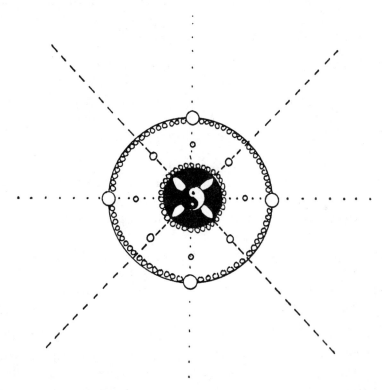

And, as I indicated in the previous chapter, the key to identifying and creating the metaphors of these archetypes is association. You associate the characters and actions you are discovering with the archetypes in the model. You determine the archetypal role they're playing in relation to the whole and bit by bit construct a paradigm. Your feelings are guiding you to that truth and you are using the model as a point of reference. Again, the important thing is to engage your feelings because that puts you in touch with your self. Then you work with those feelings until they guide you to the characters and actions you need in your model.

When you probe the fascination looking for these elements, be aggressive. Ask direct questions and seek active cooperation from your creative unconscious self. What is the entity being transformed? Who are the victims? How is the hero lured into the adventure? What is the marvelous element? Who are the love interests and the archetypal forces that will assist and motivate and guide the hero? And who are the archetypal forces that will resist and try to thwart the hero's efforts? When you pose a question to your self, you will get an answer. It may not come that instant or even that day, but it will come eventually in the form of an image or a feeling.

Then as the archetypes begin to emerge, act as a medium. Let the energies of these archetypes express themselves through you. Let the feelings of aggression, courage, loyalty, compassion, greed, and lust come forth and personify them. If it's a Nazi, a bigot, a beautiful temptress, a positive father figure, or a T-rex, get in touch with these dimensions of your self. They're all in there somewhere. Then work with and question them. Find out what they're after and why. Keep doing this until you thoroughly understand who they are and the role they were meant to play relative to the whole. Then as each character is created from another aspect of your self, you will begin to see and feel the psychological entity being created. It's the key to creating great characters and an excellent way of getting in touch with your self.

This first creative stage is the equivalent of doing research. You are inventing all of the details you would be discovering in your research, if it were a true story. Then you play with these images and ideas until you truly understand the subject (value) being explored and what you want to say. After you know what you want to say, you gradually take control of the process. It is a major turning point in the progress of your work. You go from being a simple medium to a master craftsperson and you become very adept at evolving the archetypes and their dominant traits and in revealing the hidden truth.

The Value Being Pursued

There is no particular order in which ideas will occur to you or associations will be made, but one of the first things you will probably want to discover in the fascination is the **value** you are going to explore—the value being the objective (life, health, justice, freedom, etc.) that will be pursued on the upside of the cycle. Its opposite (death, disease, injustice, slavery, etc.) is the **scourge** being created on the downside. When you explore and model that subject, you will, in effect, be describing how these values are created and destroyed. And what you have to say will be about that subject, so it should be something that really fascinates you. In *Armageddon*, the value being pursued is life and the scourge being avoided is death. The life of everyone on Earth is threatened. In *The Silence of the Lambs*, it's also a matter of life and death but on a much smaller scale. In *Mulan* and *Braveheart*, it's freedom and slavery.

The Entity Being Transformed

The entity being transformed can be any entity you like that you can draw a circle around and create archetypal equations for. Consider a lot of different arenas and wait until the fascination guides you to a place or group that really intrigues you, then gradually evolve it into your own world, your own Camelot, Chinatown, or Metropolis. Create a world that people will want to escape to. Fill it with precious objects, a marvelous atmosphere, and people you really care about, people whose inner depths you really want to explore. Ross MacDonald created a view of Los Angeles no one had seen before. Dashell Hammett created a San Francisco that belonged to Sam Spade; Sir Arthur Conan Doyle, a London that belonged to Sherlock Holmes; William Faulkner, a fictional county in Mississippi; and George Lucas, a galaxy ruled by the Force. Creating a world that hasn't been seen before will give a critical freshness and appeal to your ideas.

The State of Misfortune

Again, whether the problem (the **state of misfortune**) you discover is an effect of tyranny, a criminal act, poverty, slavery, injustice, or an alien invasion, let it be something that really fascinates or concerns you and that you want to say something about or explore. Then make the treatment of it interesting and different. Look at the problem from a different angle than we've seen before. And make the victims or potential victims beings we'll feel sympathy for, beings who can arouse our compassion and our outrage, reawaken our humanity, dissolve our inauthentic states, and make us long to become heroes again. In *A Thousand and One Nights*, it is the nightly mistresses of the king who are being beheaded. In *The Silence of the Lambs*, it's the young murder victims that have been mutilated and skinned alive. In *Mulan* and *Braveheart*, it's the current and potential victims of a brutal invader. In *The Count of Monte Cristo* and *The Fugitive*, the victims are the falsely accused heroes.

To create a **high concept**, use ideas everyone can relate to and the average person can understand, and add an intriguing **hook**, which is the aspect of the subject we haven't seen before. In *Armageddon*, the problem is very dramatic: an asteroid is about to collide with Earth. That's a very high concept, something everyone can immediately relate to and understand. The hook is the fact that the asteroid is the size of Texas, which means there will be no survivors. It is definitely over for every living thing. Action obviously has to be taken.

The Cause of the Problem

In *Armageddon*, the **cause of the problem** is the asteroid. In *The Silence of the Lambs*, it's a serial killer. In *The Lion King*, it's a usurping uncle. In *A Thousand and One Nights*, it's a disillusioned, women-distrusting king.

The cause doesn't have to be a manmade evil. A tornado, a volcano, an iceberg, or a tidal wave can represent a psychological threat just as well as a living being can. But whatever the cause, you have to feel the force of the threat and the danger. The problem has to be significant enough to attract our interest and attention, if it is to ring true. Otherwise, it's not fairly representing the unconscious, which is in reality a serious potential threat to consciousness until you learn how to manage and transform its energy.

The Holdfast/Antihero

After you discover the cause of the problem, sketch out **the downside** of the cycle. How did Darth Vader come over to the dark side? How did Hannibal Lecter become such a serious psychopath? What brilliant minds or tragic flaws brought T-rex and Frankenstein back to life? Then see if you can trace or relate the cause of the problem back to the center of the entity. If the **holdfast** commanding that position is not a dedicated criminal or tyrant, is there nevertheless a dangerous corruption, complacency, ignorance, or neglect somewhere in the background? We need to know what really caused the problem. We need to identify some of the negative energies that are responsible, bring them out into the open and personify them.

In *Jaws*, the threat comes from the shark, but the mayor of Balboa Island is practically a co-conspirator. Without his denial and his greed, would the devastating aggression on the part of the shark have been possible? In *The Silence of the Lambs*, are the negative energies personified by the warden of the prison that houses Hannibal Lecter somehow responsible for that type of criminal behavior? In the better gangster movies of the '40s, they always traced the real cause of criminal behavior back to the society itself. In *Ordinary People*, it's traced back to the mother.

The Solution to the Problem

Now, what is the **solution to the problem**? In *Armageddon*, they have to destroy or divert the asteroid. In *A Thousand and One Nights*, it's the transformation of the king. In *The Silence of the*

Lambs, they have to catch the serial killer. In *The Lion King*, Simba has to find the courage to return to Pride Rock and reclaim his throne. In *Titanic*, the solution to the problem is the same as all solutions to problems caused by natural disasters (other than an asteroid the size of Texas), and that is escape.

The Marvelous Element

And what is the **marvelous element**, the thing without which the problem can't be solved or the state of misfortune reversed? In *Armageddon*, it's a nuclear device in an eight hundred foot shaft drilled into the surface of the asteroid hurtling toward the earth at 22,000 miles an hour. In *A Thousand and One Nights*, it's a string of great stories. In *The Silence of the Lambs*, it's a profile of the serial killer that can help locate and identify him. In *Ordinary People*, it's the secret behind the young boy's suicidal tendencies. In *Titanic*, it's the lifeboats, which, unfortunately, can't hold everybody.

There are tremendous advantages to having such an element in your story, to have everything hinge on the hero achieving, discovering, or retrieving some critical element which is extremely difficult or even dangerous to accomplish or obtain. Like the principal action itself, it can help focus your objectives, unify the action, justify all of the resistance, make clear what everyone is doing and bring about the transformation. This is definitely a dimension that is worth mastering.

If the power you need is a supernatural good or evil quality, you can create the marvelous or terrible element by associating it with an object. The Holy Grail has power because it is associated with Christ consciousness; the Hope Diamond, because it is associated with an evil curse; evidence, because it is associated with the power to convict a criminal. A dagger that belonged to Genghis Khan or sneakers that belonged to Michael Jordan would take on the good or bad qualities we associate with those people.

If you have difficulty working out any of these dimensions, go back to the original fascination, which is now in the context of an entity, and work with that. As always, try a lot of different ideas and listen to your feelings. Your feelings are helping you make all the necessary decisions. Your feelings are guiding you to the truth. Everything you do creatively—every change, every new element, every new idea, every new selection or configuration—has a feeling connotation. It will feel either good or bad and you will make your decisions accordingly.

The Hero

Who is the **hero**? Whose responsibility is it to solve the problem? In *A Thousand and One Nights*, it's Scheherazade, the king's next victim. In *The Silence of the Lambs*, it's Jodie Foster acting for the FBI. In *Mulan*, it's the Emperor and his army in the *whole story* and a young girl posing as one of the Emperor's soldiers in the story focus. In *Armageddon*, this dubious distinction is given to Bruce Willis (Harry Stamper) and his crew and the astronauts who assist them. In *Scrooge*, it's the three ghosts. In *Ordinary People*, it's the psychiatrist.

The heroes don't have to be professional doctors, lawyers, or detectives; they can be ordinary citizens carrying out that ego function in an unofficial capacity (*Lorenzo's Oil*).

The Inauthentic State

Is the hero ready, or is he or she in an **inauthentic state**? In *Armageddon*, Bruce Willis is ready. In *The Silence of the Lambs*, Jodie Foster is just about ready. She just has a few small problems, which concern her dead father and some crying lambs, to work out. In *Titanic*, Leonardo DiCaprio has fallen into the problem and has no choice. But he acts instinctively and is equal to the task. In *The Lion King*, Simba is totally unprepared. And a good part of the story is about resolving that inauthentic state. In *Toy Story*, Buzz Lightyear is in a curious state of enchantment. He believes he really is a space warrior and is denying that he's just a toy.

If the hero is in an inauthentic state, you have to resolve that first (*Casablanca*), or as you go (*The Verdict*, *Toy Story*). But once he or she is taking heroic action, strive to create a definitive portrait of that professional function—i.e., make the hero not just an okay spy but a great spy, a great warrior, a great doctor. Get in touch with that ego function, with the part of your conscious self that has that responsibility and work with it creatively. Identify the virtues of that function, artistically treat them, and monitor your feelings. It will teach you what that type of hero (or ego function) really does, and give you a little of the special training your hero will need to accomplish his or her goal. Your hero will then become a psychological role model. That will make an important psychological connection and add significantly to the power of your work. The truer a hero is to the ego-archetype he or she represents, the greater the impact that hero will have.

The Archetypes of the Creative Unconscious

Now, probe the fascination and develop the other major players, the **forces of assistance and resistance.** As in real life, these archetypes are realized to the extent they are helping or hindering the hero. Their actions toward the hero reveal and define their characters. The hero walks past a doorman entering a building and the doorman doesn't react. That doorman has no character. He is just part of the atmosphere. But the moment the doorman steps in front of the hero, blocks his way, puts his hand on his chest and says, "Hey! Where do you think you're going?" he becomes a character, a force of resistance, a threshold guardian, a negative energy the hero has to overcome. This is true of all of the unconscious archetypes. Find out what role they are playing relative to the hero, and you will discover their characters.

Set the rivalry up like a game and make it fun. Remember the power that is in that rivalry, that game. The best way to teach is to make the learning fun and there is no better example of this in the universe than story.

Also, the heavies don't have to be archvillains. There are plenty of antagonists in *The Iliad* but no real villains. No truly evil people. No one person seems more virtuous than the rest. Victor

McLaglen in *The Quiet Man* is like that. He is an antagonist, not a villain. Antagonists are legitimate adversaries. They have a legitimate beef. Villains are antagonists that have a shadow side. They personify something that was repressed and has turned nasty and compulsive. And they don't play by the rules; they break the law. They do evil, antisocial things to gain their ends.

The **dominant traits** of the characters are revealed by the **choices** they make. Whether the characters are honest or dishonest, loyal or disloyal, generous or greedy, selfish or altruistic, is determined by the choices they make. One character refuses a bribe, the other accepts it. Their choices define their character. Character is built up bit by bit by these choices. Robert McKee says that deep character is revealed by choices made under pressure. By our reckoning, the deep character that will be revealed under pressure on the upside of the passage by the hero and the other positive archetypes will be good, and the deep character revealed under pressure on the downside by the antihero and the other negative archetypes will be bad.

The dominant trait should, of course, be in the context of a full human being and be largely camouflaged. If you just play the dominant trait and leave out the rest, you create stereotypes and clichés. The more human and colorful the antagonists are, the better. Siskel and Ebert praised a James Bond villain called Largo (played by Klaus Maria Brandauer) because he was not just a one-dimensional megalomaniac who wants to rule the world. Real people are full of contradictions, inner conflicts, hopes, dreams, foibles, despairs, combinations of good and bad strengths and weaknesses. In a well-drawn character, we should see all of these qualities, as you do in John Milton's Satan in *Paradise Lost* and Frank Langella's portrayal of Dracula. Audiences love well-rounded, fully realized characters, especially villains.

Another important dimension of a great character is **style**. When two characters are otherwise alike, style sets them apart and further defines their characters. The difference between Sherlock

Holmes, Charlie Chan, and Hercule Poirot, all of whom have the same dominant trait (deductive reasoning), is largely a matter of style. Holmes's approach is methodical, Chan's is intuitive, Poirot's is fastidious. These are interesting and worthwhile distinctions, and we see these styles reflected in the way they dress, the way they walk, the way they comb their hair. Giving your characters style means understanding them, and yourself, on yet another level.

Conflict

Not just the main opposing forces but all of the elements, both positive and negative, should be in conflict. Everyone has their own agenda. They all have needs—just like the organs of the body which are working together but have their individual chemical and nutritional needs. They all have the same objective but different points of view concerning what the priorities are and how each goal can be achieved.

The characters who help may resist getting involved and may need to be convinced. The hero and the love interest may have different opinions concerning how to solve the problem. They have to learn how to work together. All of the negative forces also have their separate agendas which bring them into conflict. All of this reflects the inner conflicts that are always with us.

In any case, it is always more dramatic when people are at odds than in ready agreement. But it has to be meaningful conflict, not just conflict for the sake of conflict. It has to ring true psychologically. In Hollywood, it is well known that conflict is important, but frequently the conflict is just gratuitous, two people bickering endlessly about everything and anything. The two brothers in a movie called *Backdraft* had this problem. They were constantly at each other's throats, but it was forced and it wasn't advancing the story. So let it be a real conflict of interest stemming from deeply held convictions or important needs. Get in touch with the reasons for conflict and the conflicts within yourself and personify that.

Sometimes characters who start off opposing the hero are transformed along the way. That's good because it expresses the psychological truth that all negatives are transformable into positives. There's also a possible virtue if the good guys and the bad guys know each other. It reflects a personal relationship which is psychologically true. Psychologically, we have an important relationship with the negative forces inside us. They are all related. These forces may appear like strangers at first, but later we find out there's a connection. In Charles Dickens's novels, the villain is frequently an evil relative who is trying to cheat the hero out of his fortune or do him harm. *Hamlet* and *The Lion King* are other important examples. Also, if it's necessary to utterly destroy the archvillain because he's just too evil, it might be valuable to have dupes or henchmen who can be rehabilitated. That will ring true psychologically, because the negative forces that are hidden beneath the shadow can be transformed into something positive (Valerie Perrine in *Superman*, Ben Johnson in *Shane*).

The Steps of the Passage

When you sketch out the **steps of the passage**, they don't have to be in great detail. They can just be the **essential steps**. Nor does the hero have to experience every stage. Not everyone will be affected by anger and inflation, and so forth. But you need to know how the hero got involved and what the incentives were. And you need to know how the hero was initiated, who the people were that helped and guided him or her, how the problem was solved, what happens after the climax of the initiation, and how everything is resolved. Probe the fascination of the essential steps you already have, and that will help you find the steps in between. But don't try to build major structures too early in the process. Structure has power, and once it's in place, you might not want to take it apart anymore than you would want to reframe your house. So don't let the structure jell. Gather as much raw data as you can and work with it, but be flexible and open to change. Keep everything in a fluid state. Let nothing be tied down. Everything is a reference point that can lead to other, better ideas. When it stops evolving, it stops growing.

Camouflage

All of the symbolic elements, of course, have to be hidden. There are big points off, if the audience realizes it is watching something symbolic. It becomes an allegory, which is the lowest form of story metaphor and an intellectual rather than emotional experience. In the film *The Natural*, Darren McGavin has a big glass eye, the evil woman wears black, the good woman wears white, and you're saying to yourself, "Gee, all of this must mean something." It's very distracting. On the other hand, when you're watching *Dracula* or *Jaws*, you're never deflected by the thought that it means something. You're experiencing the metaphor through your feelings, not your intellect. You encounter the images, respond emotionally, and absorb their meaning unconsciously. You don't have to think about it and it has a profound and lasting effect.

Sometimes authors don't even know that they are creating a metaphor. Herman Melville denied until he died that Moby Dick had any symbolic meaning. It was just a story, he insisted. But that's too bad. The equation created by Ahab, the ship, the great white whale, and the ocean have a psychological significance whether he likes it or not. If you work correctly, this could easily happen. In other words, you don't really have to understand what your story metaphor means, only how it feels. If it feels right, it means something, even if you don't understand what that something is. So let it be an adventure of discovery and take comfort in the fact that you are not working alone. The source of those positive and negative feelings is a serious partner. Be patient and have faith in the process. You're in the business of discovering and revealing the truth.

CHAPTER 28

STORY ALCHEMY

After you've sketched out your model and know what you want to say, the second creative stage will gradually take over. This stage is dominated by the last three creative techniques—**conjuring, testing,** and **problem solving**—and is designed to help you create and evolve a perfect metaphor of the hidden truth.

The artistic tools at work here are **analysis** and **recombination, exaggeration** and **miniaturization, idealization** and **vilification.** You are taking things apart and trying this character and scene here and that character and incident there. You are changing the relationships, altering the relative sizes and strengths and making the positive things better and the negative things worse. You keep in constant touch with your feelings and wait for the creative unconscious to send you insights and signals.

Every creative playing or conjuring is a question to your self. You are in effect asking your self: Is it like this? The feeling response you get is your answer. And you keep playing with the creative ideas until they come out just right, until they really work.

Take Dracula, for instance. You're trying to find something your characters can use to repel him. The first thing you try are rosary beads and you're monitoring your feelings. You imagine Dracula coming toward you with an evil intent. You hold up the beads to repel him but nothing happens. He pushes them aside and goes for your throat. So you try the Bible. Again nothing happens. Another dud. Finally, you try the cross—and, ahhh! you get a chill up your spine and Dracula shrinks back. Something inside you is saying: That's it.

The asteroid in *Armageddon* may have started out as an ordinary meteor only three miles in diameter. That didn't work too well so they tried one the size of the moon. That was too big so they kept at it until it reached its present form, which they knew was right because of the way it felt. In Disney's *Hercules*, Hades may have started out like the usual Satan without the burning hair, which was realized later. The burning hair that changes color with Hades' moods is brilliant and must have felt extremely good when it was discovered.

And what's true for the characters and marvelous elements is true for the scenes and the arrangement of the scenes. You evolve everything to its ultimate, quintessential form. You keep working until you create a brilliant solution to your problem and find the ideal arrangement for your scenes. The more intriguing, fascinating, and awe-inspiring everything is, the closer you are getting to the truth.

Words on Paper

When you start working with words on paper or on a computer screen instead of just images in your head, you continue with this same evolutionary process—revising, editing, rearranging, rewriting. These are all forms of **conjuring**. It's what the creative process is all about.

The first things you put down on paper are liable to be very disappointing. But don't get discouraged. It's how the creative process works. Visual images and feelings, especially those with real power, are complex, marvelous, and mysterious things. So to find just the right words to express them is bound to be difficult, requiring a great deal of effort, a great deal of trial and error, a great deal of conjuring, a long creative dialogue with your creative unconscious self.

In any case, don't just stare at a blank page, put something down. A bad idea on paper is much better than no idea, because a bad idea is an excellent reference point. It can help you find what you're looking for. Put ten bad ideas on the page, and you'll know ten things that are not what you're looking for. And if you know ten things it's not, then what it should be will soon reveal itself.

Trial and error, as always, is the key. Just keep working and let your feelings guide you through the process. Until you get to the end, everything is only a temporary reference point to help lead you to other, more powerful ideas. You just keep exploring and conjuring, and listening to your feelings, waiting for something really powerful to emerge. Then you start probing these new, more fascinating ideas until even more powerful fascinations emerge. Eventually you'll strike gold.

The proof of all this is that your work will be noticeably better with every evolution. Every change adds energy to the process.

Modern Metaphors and the Hidden Truth

To make metaphors modern and **relevant**, just utilize modern, contemporary elements of today's idiom. Be aware of contemporary interests and preoccupations; start with those real things— contemporary people, actions, situations, artifacts, etc.—and treat them artistically. When you artistically treat, recombine, and reassociate these contemporary things, you'll get the same effects as the old metaphors, but they will be things that modern people can easily relate to. To make metaphors **fresh** you have to come up with unique combinations, variations we haven't seen before. Your feelings will tell you when you've chosen a metaphor that makes a psychological connection. You know when something is right or not by how you feel about it. The acid test is always "what works," what gets your juices going. The more powerful the feeling, the closer you are getting to the truth.

And that's the fourth great secret contained in this book. When you're conjuring creative ideas and you make a correspondence with the hidden truth, you will get a confirmation. It will give you goose flesh. When you hit upon the right combinations, it will let you know. If you create a character, an action, or a marvelous element that contains hidden truth, you will get a confirmation, a feeling that it "works." The more conjuring you do, the more writing and rewriting you do, the more confirmations you will experience. The more confirmations you experience, the more hidden truth you will incorporate into your story and the more power it will have. This is how you tease the truth to the surface. And this is how you steal fire from the gods.

Charisma

And when the characters and events actually make the psychological connection and become metaphors of the hidden truth, they become charismatic, which is to say, symbolic. People will be attracted to them and influenced by them even if they don't know what they mean. The strength of the **charisma** is brought about by the degree of fidelity to the hidden truth behind the archetypes. The more faithfully the metaphors personify this hidden truth, the more powerful and charismatic the effect. The increase in fidelity is brought about by conjuring. It is the key to making your characters truly memorable (and merchandizable).

Characters that possess this charisma become like deities. Oedipus, Moses, Zeus, Jesus, Achilles, Krishna, Hamlet, Romeo and Juliet, and King Arthur are unforgettable, and Chaplin's tramp, Rhett Butler, Dorothy, E.T., Dracula, Mickey Mouse, and Superman are definitely steps in the right direction. Put Superman on a little boy's pajamas and it makes him feel stronger. He'll try to fly around the room. Put Nala on a little girl's sneakers and it makes her feel frisky and ready for an adventure. Put Einstein on your T-shirt and it will make you feel smarter. Put Ghengis Khan on your leather jacket and you're ready for a Harley. That's charisma.

CHAPTER 29

CREATING THE STORY FOCUS

After you've worked with the whole cycle for a while and you've got something really hot, you can begin thinking about the **focus** of your story. The **theme** of the focus will be the aspect of the subject (value) you want to explore. You can explore any place you like in as much depth as you like, so long as it involves some major or minor problem-solving action that is essential to the progress of the whole passage. Explore a number of different possibilities, then select the one you ultimately find the most intriguing and compelling. You can do a full sweep of the major actions on the upside, from the hero's getting involved to the climax of the initiation or some small piece of that action. Or you can focus on the transformation of the hero, on some aspect of the aftermath (III) or the return (IV). Or you can focus on the downside and create another *Godfather* or *Macbeth*.

In *Armageddon*, the problem of the story focus is the same as the problem of the *whole story* (an asteroid the size of Texas is going to collide with Earth and destroy all life). In *Mulan* and *The Silence of the Lambs* it is also the same. Usually, the problem is not the same when you are focusing on the transformation of the hero or the antihero (*The Grapes of Wrath*). When the principal action is the same, then the resolution of the hero's inauthentic state is integrated into the main action (*The Verdict*).

The narrower the focus, the more depth and subtlety. The broader the stroke, the more action, the less depth. And whatever focus you choose, you will then tell the rest of the *whole story* through that vantage point. If the *whole story* is not known, if it's not a historical event like World War II, then you have to indicate in the afterthought how the fictional *whole story* you are creating will end. If you choose a time when everything is coming to a head, the power of the entire circle can be realized through that one focal point. The whole wheel can come rushing through that one point in a powerful and entertaining way—as it does in *The Iliad* and *Death of a Salesman*.

Point of View

In real life, we can examine a problem not just from our own but from just about any other **point of view**. The mind can alter its point of view in a given situation and become objective. This is reflected in storymaking by the fact that having set up the **whole cycle** and the focus, you can tell the story from the point of view of any character. In Dostoyevsky's *Crime and Punishment*, there is a murder and a police investigation (a downside **inciting action** and an upside **principal action**). Most stories of this type are told from the point of view of the police investigator. Dostoyevsky tells his story from the point of view of the murderer. The movies *Taxi Driver* and Fritz Lang's *M* do the same. In *Titanic*, the focus is the same as the *whole story* (an unsinkable ship hits an iceberg) but the story is told from the point of view of Leonardo DiCaprio and Kate Winslet, star-crossed lovers who just happen to be on board. As long as you can see the *whole story* in the background, you can focus on anyone's point of view that you choose.

The Structures of the Principal Action

After you've selected the story focus, and the problem of the focus, then determine which actions and scenes belong to the **inciting action** and **principal action** and which actions will be revealed in the **exposition** and **afterthought**.

After that isolate the principal action and divide it into the essential actions (solution formula) that will help the hero to **identify**, **locate**, **confront**, and **transform** the cause of the problem.

The most important of these action threads will be the **dominant plot**. The objective of the dominant plot will determine the **genre**. Then probe the relevant fascinations of these actions to determine which actions belong to which subplots (this will also clue you in to the types of feelings those scenes should arouse). Then if you interrelate the plots and subplots and make them interdependent, you will create a metaphor of how the mind works and add that power to your story.

Then continue to probe the relevant fascinations until you discover which actions are creating the **complications, crises,** and **climaxes** in each of these plots. Each of these large and small action threads, from the principal action on down, will be driven by the trial-and-error process and have a **classical structure.** The act structure will generally follow the classical structure of the dominant plot.

The most important of these classical elements is the **crisis** of the dominant plot, because that is the event that forces the hero to make the sacrifice (or decision) that frees the power (or the knowledge) that is necessary to climax the action. The main crisis is also the true middle or center of the story. If you track the action, by cause and effect, forward from the beginning, it will take you to the crisis and no further. If you track the action, by cause and effect, backwards from the end, it will also take you to the crisis and no further. That is because the crisis, which is in the center or middle of the story, contains a major change of direction (**turning point**). The crisis is, in fact, the only vantage point from which you can comfortably survey the entire story focus. If you imagine yourself at the crisis, you can see in both directions, back to the beginning or forward to the climax.

The dominant plot of *Armageddon* is a war story, a physical battle with an asteroid that will end in either victory or defeat. But in order to succeed in that difficult mission NASA has to have the cooperation of the designated heroes (emotional subplot), and in order to get their cooperation, they have to come up with some very convincing ideas (mental subplot). The other emotional subplots all have to do with the emotional conflicts Harry has with his daughter, Grace, her boyfriend, A.J., the other members of his crew, and the NASA personnel, all of which also have to be worked out if the mission is to succeed. The other mental subplots have to do with the mathematical and astrophysical puzzles that have to be mastered in order to reach the asteroid and survive. The spiritual subplot has to do with the immortalization of Harry. When he sacrifices himself for his daughter and saves the world, he is instantly deified. The crisis of the dominant, physical plot occurs when the nuclear device won't detonate automatically and someone has to stay behind. The climax of the main emotional subplot happens when Harry saves A.J. from death by taking his place. And so on.

Artistic Statement

As always, be guided by your feelings and try a lot of different ideas until you find what really works. The better it works, the closer you are getting to the truth. And if you make your scenes about one thing, then everything in that scene can serve that one objective. You can probe the fascination (core element) of that scene and create the ideal atmosphere, mood, and setting to support it, and you can make a powerful **artistic statement**. It will also greatly increase the clarity of the scene and help to focus the feelings of the audience. They will sink right into the essential feeling. The simpler the scene is, the richer you can make it. These are limitations that allow for richness of detail. The more complicated a scene is, the less effective it is because it dissipates and confuses the emotions by jumping from one feeling or idea to another. If your scenes aren't working, the first thing you should check is whether they're too complicated. If they are too complicated, then break them into simpler units, find the core element of the new units, probe their fascinations, and see if you aren't creating a far more powerful effect this way.

Dialogue

Translate everything you can into action then add as little dialogue as necessary to make clear what's happening. The most effective dialogue is the least dialogue necessary to explain the actions and express the feelings of the participants.

Great dialogue feels and sounds like real conversation, which is fascinating and full of colorful and emotionally charged patterns.

It advances the story, reveals character, and is often humorous. On the way to the airport, a New York cab driver said this to me: "When I feel captivated in New York, I think about Florida and try to picturesque it in my mind."

To make dialogue real, listen to how people really talk, and creatively adapt it. If the dialogue is genuine to begin with, it will seem real no matter how you exaggerate, shorten, or otherwise alter it. The principles of great dialogue are the laws of conversation in real life artistically treated.

A few of the things you might notice when you are observing real conversation is that people only rarely talk about what's really on their minds. They are talking about the weather, but they really want to ask for a date or get to know you better (**subtext**). People rarely discuss things in sequence. They often have several things to say and wait for an opportunity to make their point, regardless of what the other person is saying. People act differently with different people, especially if they've known them for a long time or if they've known them intimately. People rarely give straight answers but talk indirectly (**indirection**). I overheard this conversation on the UCLA campus. A boy with blond hair approached a second boy who was hanging out in front of Ackerman Union.

"Are you going to Tony's later?" the newcomer asked.

The second boy looked surprised. "Were you there Friday night?"

"Marty told me."

"Hey, that's great." And they connected with a high-five.

There was not a single direct answer to any of the questions, but the answers were clear from the context. Is the second boy going to Tony's later? Yes. Was the first boy there Friday night? No. Hmm. Interesting.

Narrative (Poetic) Structure

If you lay out all the actions, including past history and afterthought, in chronological order, the incidents can then be presented in almost any arrangement. (*Toto le Heros*, *Two for the Road*). You can show how the state of misfortune was established at the beginning of the story (*Jaws*) or reveal it later in the middle of the story as part of the exposition (*Casablanca*, *Scrooge*). The story can begin right before the beginning of the climactic battle (*Die Hard*) or a year after the climactic battle ends *(Parade of Ants)*. It just all has to come out right in the end. All of which implies unlimited creative possibilities.

All of the **units of action** you create can be treated artistically in the same way as the visual images. They can be taken apart, shifted around, conjured, and reassembled someplace else. You can take an ordinary sentence and work with it in this way (artistically) until it becomes a line of great poetry.*

You can work in this way with the sentences of a paragraph or the paragraphs of a chapter, shifting things around, substituting this for that, generating new ideas, selecting the most powerful, and conjuring until you have evolved the most potent combinations. This, of course, is what rewriting is all about—conjuring until the words are equal to the visual images you are trying to describe.

The emphasis you give an element will depend on its importance relative to the whole. In real life when you have a problem, you can look at any aspect of the problem in as much detail as you like. And so it is in storymaking. You can develop or give special emphasis to any part of the focus structure that you like. You can concentrate your story at a particular point and intensify it, or spread it out as much as you like. You can make the climax last two minutes or spread it out over fifteen rounds of boxing, as in *Rocky*. You can take any part of your story and intensify, deepen, or elongate it as much as you like.

---

* Look at the quote from *A Midsummer Night's Dream* at the opening of Part IV of this book. Shakespeare is saying what I'm saying, but in a far more eloquent way.

As Joseph Campbell explains it,

> "The changes rung on the simple scale of the monomyth defy description. Many tales isolate and greatly enlarge upon one or two of the typical elements of the full cycle (test motif, flight motif, abduction of the bride), others string a number of independent cycles into a single series (as in *The Odyssey*). Differing characters or episodes can become fused, or a single element can reduplicate itself and reappear under many changes."

As long as it comes full circle at the end, there are no set rules.

CHAPTER 30

THE MOZART EFFECT

In the fourth creative stage you go back over everything and if you've been working correctly, you may reach a point when the floodgates suddenly open and the right ideas are flowing so fast, you will be astounded. You will know by the way you feel that something extraordinary is happening. And when this happens, don't stop. Write as fast as you can and don't question the process or think about what's happening until it's over. If it flows for ten minutes, an hour, or a week, just let it happen. If you stop to do something else, the wave will probably have passed when you return. In any case, it doesn't happen very often, but when it does it's exhilarating.

CHAPTER 31

CREATING THE SUGAR COAT

After you've developed the focus, conjured all of the metaphors, fleshed everything out, and clearly understand what you want to say, you enter the fifth creative stage whereby you fine tune the metaphors and use the six creative techniques to subtly perfect the actions that create the sugar coat.

Each of the hundred or so powerful dimensions of a story has an impact on the sugar coat, on the entertainment values of the story, so the more dimensions you can add and perfect, the greater the emotional impact on the audience. The more substance you can put behind it, the more powerful your story is going to be—the better the audience will like it and the more often they will come back to enjoy it.

When you isolate the genre actions, you isolate the feelings associated with them. And when you conjure those genre elements and perfect them, you reveal more of the hidden truth and intensify the emotional response. The closer you get to the hidden truth, the greater the response. And if you actually reach the hidden truth, the sugar coat will go off scale.

So learn as much as you can about what an audience feels and why, and how those feelings are created. Be aware of what works for you, then figure out why it works. What just happened? What caused those feelings or that laughter? And you will quickly develop an instinct for it. If you're being guided by your feelings, all of this will happen naturally. Remember that the promise of these feelings lures them into the experience, but it also puts them in touch with themselves, with their feelings.

If you are creating a **tragedy** or a **romance**, you are exaggerating the nobility of the characters and putting the audience in touch with their true potential. You are giving them a taste of who they really are.

If you're creating a **comedy**, the basic situation will still be real, but you are isolating and exaggerating the foibles and flaws people have, the frequency with which errors occur, and the irony experienced by your characters. Woody Allen makes people laugh by exaggerating his own hypochondria and neurosis. Charlie Chaplin exaggerated the frequency with which mishaps and catastrophes can occur. Charles Dickens exaggerated the ignorance and belligerent slowness of his bureaucrats and the difficulties his heroes had in trying to deal with them, and so on. The more **laughter** you can provoke, the closer you are getting to the truth. Even serious plays like *Hamlet* have, or should have, a great deal of humor. A story without humor is not about human beings.

If you want to make people cry, separate or reunite two characters the audience cares deeply about, and that will put them in touch with the tragedy of separation deep within their own souls.

If you want to increase the **love** the audience feels toward your hero, let the hero do kind, humane, and loving things. And let him show courage and be willing to sacrifice himself for the sake of others. If you want to make the villain more villainous, isolate the negative forces and conjure them until you have thoroughly vilified him. That will intensify the loathing the audience will feel toward him and it will also intensify the rejection they will feel toward similar impulses arising in themselves.

If you want to increase the **passion** your audience is feeling, fill your characters with deep emotional feelings like passion and love and you will arouse those feelings in your audience. If the characters could care less about each other, the audience will feel the same about them. Passion is our feeling potential. It's how we should be feeling toward one another. Increasing the passion of your characters puts the audience in touch with those feelings and that hidden truth.

Audiences love it when characters show their feelings—especially **changes of heart, forgiveness, acts of kindness,** and **self-sacrifice.**

Angels with Dirty Faces is worth viewing just to see the sacrifice James Cagney makes at the end.

If you want to increase the **excitement**, isolate and artistically treat the physical action and intensify it. Raise the stakes, increase the urgency and the danger, and quicken the pace. And save the greatest burst of energy for the climax of the dominant plot. The more exciting it becomes, the closer you are getting to the truth underlying that dimension.

If you want to increase the **suspense**, make us anxious over how things will turn out and delay the result. Excite interest or curiosity, then hold back the resolution. Anything that causes tension and anxiety causes suspense if it's unrelieved. And what causes tension or anxiety? Anything intriguing or threatening that's unresolved.

The more there is at stake, the greater the tension and suspense, and the closer you are getting to that truth. And if everything is at stake and there's no time to lose, and the odds are overwhelming and success is highly unlikely, you will maximize the tension and suspense and create a perfect metaphor of what the conscious element experiences when it confronts the negative unconscious. In real life, everything is always at stake. There really is no time to lose and the outcome is always extremely uncertain. When nothing is at stake, it's not about life and there is very little tension and suspense.

As for the **aesthetic** and **technical dimensions**, you only have to realize they are important and they will begin to work for you. The moment you realize that **timing** and **variety** are important, you will begin to develop an instinct for it. And the more you work with them, the better it will become. All of these dimensions have an optimum potential, an exact, right proportion that can transform something ordinary into something incredible. And you achieve this incredible potential by creating a *golden mean*, a perfect balance between too little and too much—between too little variety, for instance, and too much variety. You play with your ideas until suddenly everything falls into place and they begin to glow and you create something so extraordinary and fine it is irresistible. As long as you keep everything in a fluid state and keep evolving it, there's no limit to the beauty you can achieve. The closer you get to the truth, the more pleasing the effect.

In summary, there are **six ways to add power to a dimension**. The first is to create a metaphor. This is accomplished by associating the elements with the archetypes. The second way is to increase the fidelity of the archetype by conjuring, by trying a hundred different combinations and listening to your feelings until you discover what really works. The pleasant result of this is charisma. The third way is to add more dimensions. Each of the hundred or so dimensions of story impacts the sugar coat, so the more dimensions you can add and perfect, the greater the emotional impact on the audience. The fourth way is to narrow the focus. The less you look at, the richer you can make what you see. The fifth way is to find the center. The fascination is the center of the story, the core element is the center of the scene, and the crisis is the center of the principal action. If you learn to work from the center, you can make a powerful artistic statement. The sixth and final way to add power is the *golden mean*, which expresses the power hidden in the aesthetic and technical dimensions and is another window through which the hidden truth is revealed.

And, hopefully, what all of this will make clear is that there is no conflict between art and entertainment. They are two aspects of the same thing. Entertainment is energized by art and purpose. The more purpose and art you can put into the story, the greater will be the entertainment effects. If you approach story solely from the point of view of entertainment, you will only scratch the surface of the entertainment possibilities and leave out all of the nutritional elements the audience desperately needs.

CHAPTER 32

THE FINAL CUT

This final creative stage is simple enough. You edit out everything you don't need and make everything you do need as short and as marvelous as possible—i.e., you reduce the number of actions to the least information necessary to describe the action, reveal meaning, and relate the parts to the whole. If you select the right highlights and find the most powerful arrangement, the delighted minds of the audience will fill in all the gaps and the effect will be magical.

CHAPTER 33

PERSEVERENCE

On the technical side, I recommend that you work with your creative ideas until you can express them as a great idea, which is to say, a high concept or an incident worth repeating, and then field-test it. It is important to put your work out there to be tested. You won't know for sure that you're tapping into something powerful and universal until you have that confirmed by outside sources. So you need to develop relationships with knowledgeable people you can trust to give you an honest reaction. That's not easy to do and it takes time, but it needs to be done. You will learn things about your work that way which you could never figure out on your own.

After you've assimilated that feedback, develop your ideas into a twenty-page treatment or oral pitch and get feedback on that. And when you've assimilated those results, then write a first draft or extended treatment and put that out there. And keep doing this until it's finished. There's no limit to the number of drafts. It's an evolutionary process and you should take the time to get it right.

And when you're finally finished, then really get your work out there. Once your work is of a professional quality, then perseverance is the key to success. You persevere until you find the allies who will help you find the agents who will help you find the producers or publishers who will help you get your work to the public. People are at different stages of development and have different needs and different tastes, so you have to find the people who share your chemistry and your vision. It takes a lot of time and effort but they're out there.

F. Scott Fitzgerald received one hundred and twenty-six pink slips from publishers rejecting his first novel, *This Side of Paradise*. The one hundred and twenty-seventh publisher accepted it and it was an overnight success. So don't start feeling discouraged until you've been rejected at least that many times. And, if you are a novelist, keep in mind that your hardcover book only has to appeal to one in a hundred readers to become a bestseller. That means that ninety-nine out of a hundred potential readers can completely ignore or dislike your work and you can still be a bestselling author. The same is true of agents, producers, and publishers. One in a hundred is enough to launch a career. So persevere.

In any case, the most important thing is a good start, so be sure to pick a project that is truly worthy of your time and talents. Nine out of ten ideas that you try out will be duds and you'll lose interest in them. Keep working until you find something that has real power, something that's really worth your time, that can sustain your interest for a year or so. And don't try to outguess or make the grade in Hollywood. Hollywood is not set up to develop talent, it's set up to exploit success. Explore the things you really want to write about and do those things in such a way that Hollywood and everyone else cannot resist them. Do something really significant and they will hunt you down.

And remember, at any given moment, you are only one great idea away from success.

CHAPTER 34

CONCLUSION

The mandate of story is very clear. With every action, in every cycle, at every stage, you are being prepared to play an important role in the world. The goal of one of these passages is the initiation of the ego so that it can absorb and manage the unconscious material and the enormous power that goes with it. We begin in an inauthentic state and we're stuck. And we have to be lured into the process. To be lured, there have to be incentives, fantasies and illusions, a little self-deception, and a promise of romance. There are commitments to be made and tasks to be accomplished. Fear barriers to be crossed and forces of resistance to be overcome. There are risks to be taken and realities to be faced. Relationships to be established and temptations to be avoided. There are feelings to be awakened and sacrifices to be made. And in the end, we have to confront and overcome our biggest fears. And then cope with inflation if our success goes to our head. And the whole thing is set up so that you can only move in one direction, like the veins in the bloodstream, which have valves that prevent the blood from moving backwards. The incentives and commitments drive us forward. The unforeseen and unanticipated events provide the problems and complications. The crisis provides the solution. And in the end, we discover we were equal to the task.

The principal elements—the entity being transformed, the state of misfortune, the cause and the solution, the principal action, the marvelous element, the change of fortune—these are all things straight out of our lives. We are the entity being transformed, the state of misfortune is our discontent, there is a cause and a solution, the principal action is what we have to do to change our fortune, and the marvelous element is the most important thing we have to achieve to make that happen. If we make the right commitments and choices, we will be guided and assisted the whole way. But we have to do it ourselves and there's no turning back. Refusing the call or turning back are the stuff that tragedies and empty lives are made of. So listen to your dreams, make the commitment, and take action.

> "The teller of stories has everywhere and always found eager listeners. Whether his tale is the mere report of a recent happening, a legend of long ago, or an elaborately contrived fiction, men and women have hung upon his words and satisfied their yearnings for information or amusement, for incitement to heroic deeds, for religious edification, or for release from the overpowering monotony of their lives. In villages of central Africa, in outrigger boats on the Pacific, in the Australian bush, and within the shadow of Hawaiian volcanoes, tales of the present and of the mysterious past, of animals and gods and heroes, and of men and women like themselves, hold listeners in their spell or enrich the conversation of daily life. So it is also in Eskimo igloos under the light of seal-oil lamps, in the tropical jungles of Brazil, and by the totem poles of the British Columbian coast. In Japan too, and China and India, the priest and the scholar, the peasant and the artisan all join in their love of a good story and their honor for the person who tells it well."
>
> Stith Thompson, *The Folktale*

I began by saying there are six billion people in the world with a desperate need for real stories which isn't being met. Give the world something it desperately needs and the world will heap treasures and honors upon you beyond your wildest dreams.

Give the world something it desperately needs.

Give it great stories.

"The way to defend art is to produce it."

Edward Cerny

EPILOGUE

I take a serious interest in your storymaking futures. Everything I know or come to know, you will know, if you're interested. So let us know who you are. You can write me in care of the publisher, seek out our website at *www.storymaking.com*, or e-mail us at *Bonnet@storymaking.com*.

photo by Zachary Holland

If you run across books or ideas we should be aware of, let us know. And if you're interested in our seminars or our consulting services, or if you would like to be on our mailing list, let us know that, too. There's a revolution taking place in the world of storymaking and you could be a part of it.

James Bonnet

Astoria Filmwrights

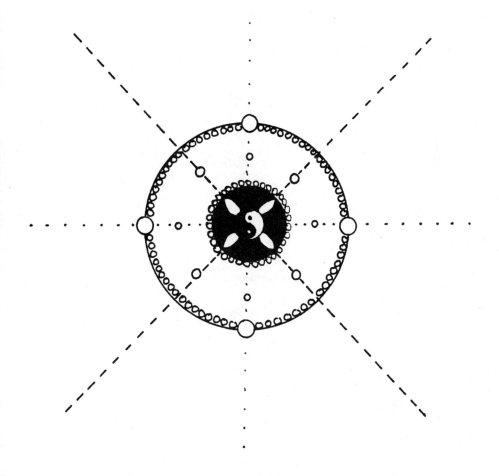

BIBLIOGRAPHY

Bettelheim, Bruno. *The Uses of Enchantment.* New York: Alfred A. Knopf, 1976.

Butcher, S. H. *Aristotle's Theory of Poetry and Fine Art.* New York: Dover, 1951.

Campbell, Joseph. *The Hero with a Thousand Faces.* Princeton, New Jersey: Princeton University Press, 1973.

Edinger, Edward F. *Ego and Archetype.*: Baltimore, Maryland: Pelican, 1974.

Estes, Clarissa Pinkola. *Women Who Run with the Wolves.* New York: Ballantine, 1992.

Jung, C. G. *The Archetypes and the Collective Unconscious.* New York: Bollingen/Pantheon, 1959.

May, Rollo. *The Courage to Create.* New York: Bantam, 1975.

Neumann, Erich. *Art and the Creative Unconscious.* New York: Bollingen/Pantheon, 1959.

Neumann, Erich. *The Origins and History of Consciousness.* New York: Bollingen/ Pantheon, 1954.

Samuels, Shorter, and Plaut. *A Critical Dictionary of Jungian Analysis.* London and New York: Routledge & Kegan Paul,1987.

Thompson, Stith. *The Folktale.* Berkeley: University of California Press, 1977.

Zimmer, Heinrich. *Myths and Symbols in Indian Art and Civilization.* New York: Harper Torchbooks, 1962.

GLOSSARY

action: The physical activities that make up the incidents of a story.

aesthetic dimensions: Pleasing effects like clarity, beauty, elegance, harmony, rhythm, and grace that are created by the **technical dimensions**.

afterthought: One of the structures of the **story focus**, it links the focus to the **whole story** by pointing to events in the future that will affect the *whole story*'s outcome.

alienation: A stage on the **downside** of the **passage** wherein the **holdfast** and the **antihero** take actions which bring about a disintegration of personality. Compare **integration**.

anima: An **archetype** of the **creative unconscious self** that expresses the feminine aspect at work in the man's **psyche**.

animus: An **archetype** of the **creative unconscious self** that expresses the masculine aspect at work in the woman's **psyche**.

antagonist: A character who opposes the **protagonist** or main character.

anti-classic: A story on the **downside** of the **storywheel** that reveals how the individual is alienated from the society in which he or she lives. Compare **classic**.

anti–fairy tale: A story on the **downside** of the **storywheel** that reveals how the individual is alienated from himself or herself. Compare **fairy tale**.

antihero: The negative, dark side of the hero. The central character in a story that ends tragically on the **downside**.

antihero's journey: The **antihero**'s progress through the **downside** of the **passage**.

anti-legend: A story on the **downside** of the **storywheel** that reveals how the individual is alienated from the world at large. Compare **legend**.

anti-myth: A story on the **downside** of the **storywheel** that reveals how the individual is alienated from the spiritual or cosmic self. Compare **myth**.

archetypes: The psychic energies revealed by the recurring patterns (**metaphors**) found in **great stories**, **myths**, and dreams. The model created from these archetypal patterns creates a rough sketch of the **hidden truth**.

artistic statement: A powerful aesthetic effect that can be created when a scene has only one objective.

artistic tools of the imagination: The curious tendencies of the mind that drive the natural storymaking process: analysis, recombination, exaggeration, miniaturization, idealization, vilification, etc. By altering the relative size, composition, or strength of story elements, the **storymaker** can create **metaphors** that more exactly reveal the **hidden truth**.

attachment: A stage on the **downside** of the **passage** wherein the **holdfast** and the **antihero** are drawn into the darkside.

backstory: That part of the story which is off-camera and revealed by the **exposition**.

camouflage: The **imitations of real life**, revelations of **character**, and **entertainment dimensions** that help a **great story** conceal its **hidden truth**.

central character: The main character in a story, frequently but not always the hero.

change of fortune: The cycles of good and bad fortune being created by the **passages** of the **Golden Paradigm**.

character: A player in a story. The sum of a person's moral qualities; their unique stamp.

character archetypes: The principal characters in a story which are the **metaphors** that represent the **archetypes** of the **conscious** and **creative unconscious self**—the **ego/hero**, the positive and negative **physical, emotional, mental,** and **spiritual** archetypes, the **anima, animus, threshold guardian, trickster,** and **shadow.**

charisma: The magnetic effect created by a **metaphor** that is making a powerful psychological connection.

choices: The choices a person makes reveal their **dominant traits** and **character.**

classic: A story on the **upside** of the **storywheel** that relates the individual to the society in which he or she lives.

classical structure: The structure of problem-solving action in real life and the **essence of story.** Its components are **complications, reversal, crisis, discovery, climax,** and **resolution.**

climax: The climactic actions necessary to bring about a solution. See **classical structure.**

comedy: A story that exaggerates the foibles and misadventures of its characters and ends happily. Compare **tragedy, romance, drama.**

complications: Risks and difficulties encountered in problem solving. See **classical structure.**

comparing and selecting: A **creative technique** whereby you save the ideas that provoke the strongest positive feelings and discard the rest.

complex: The archetypes of the **creative unconscious self** are divisible into subordinate functions called complexes.

conflict: The natural struggle for influence, supremacy, and control that exists in the real world and between the different **conscious** and **unconscious** dimensions of our psyche.

conjuring: A **creative technique** in which emerging metaphors are evolved into more perfect reflections of the underlying archetypes.

conscious self: All of the things we are consciously aware of—our thoughts, feelings, mental images, etc.

core element: The center or **fascination** of a **scene.** What the scene is about.

creative process: The method used by storymakers to fashion great stories.

creative techniques: The creative process described in this book utilizes six creative techniques—**probing the fascination, comparing and selecting, modeling, conjuring, testing,** and **problem solving.**

creative unconscious self: The source of all the higher, universal intelligence and wisdom we possess. Potential consciousness. The **hidden truth.** The **archetypes** of the creative unconscious self guide us through the **passages** of the **Golden Paradigm** and are responsible for bringing potential consciousness to consciousness.

crisis: The apparent defeat of our best efforts in problem solving. See **classical structure.**

curious tendencies of the mind: See **artistic tools of the imagination.**

cycle: See **passage.**

death: A stage on the **downside** of the **passage** wherein the **holdfast** and the **antihero** take actions which destroy the spirit and deaden consciousness. Compare **rebirth.**

dialogue: The words spoken in a story. The principles of great dialogue are the laws of conversation in real life artistically treated.

215

discovery: An insight that can lead to a solution in problem solving. See **classical structure**.

dominant plot: A story's most significant, dramatic action.

dominant trait: The outstanding quality a character personifies—i.e., greed, lust, loyalty, anger, etc.

downside: The dark, negative half of the **passage**. Compare **upside**.

drama: A serious story which can end happily or unhappily and presents its characters as they are generally found in real life. Compare **tragedy, comedy, romance**.

dynamic cycle: The energy cycles of the **Golden Paradigm**. The rivalry between the **higher** and **lower self** to control the destiny of the entity is the engine that drives the cycles of transformation.

ego: The center of consciousness.

ego/hero archetype: The positive, constructive energies of the creative conscious mind. See **nascent ego** and **hero**.

emotional: The part of our selves that manages social affairs and feelings.

emotional archetypes: The **archetypes** created by the energies of the emotional brain (**limbic system**) and the source of our social feelings. In great stories, they are the positive and negative emotional father and mother figures.

emphasis: The relative importance given to a story element.

entertainment dimensions: The pleasant sensations an audience feels when it experiences a good story. Passion, suspense, excitement, magic, laughter and tears, fear, enchantment, and surprise are among the most significant and enjoyable.

entity being transformed: A unified human group (i.e., government, tribe, corporation, etc.) that can act in story as a **metaphor** of the **psyche**.

essence of story: That without which there would be no story. See **classical structure**.

evil: The uncontrolled or misguided expression of instinctual impulses that promote antisocial or illegal behavior.

exaggeration: An **artistic tool of the imagination**.

exposition: A structure of the **story focus** that links the focus to the **whole story** by revealing events that occurred outside the frame of the story being told.

fairy tale: A story on the **upside** of the **storywheel** that relates individuals to themselves or their family, or otherwise prepares them for life. This category includes all stories of childhood and youth, not just traditional fairy tales.

fantasy: An artistic treatment of the real world that reveals the **hidden truth**.

fascination: An idea or visual image that provokes strong feelings and inspires you to create a story.

fear barrier: A fear threshold that has to be crossed by the **hero** to complete the **passage**.

feelings: One of the important ways the **creative unconscious self** communicates with the **conscious self**.

focus: See **story focus**.

forces of assistance: The positive **archetypes** on the **upside**. The negative archetypes on the **downside**. Compare **forces of resistance**.

forces of resistance: The positive **archetypes** on the **downside**. The negative archetypes on the **upside**. Compare **forces of assistance**.

frame story: See whole story.

genre: The feeling quality given to an action or dominant plot by the emotional, physical, mental, or spiritual character of its objective.

genre structure: The interacting plots and subplots of a principal action that reveal how the heart, mind, body, and soul work together. See genre.

Golden Paradigm: A model of the psyche created by patterns discovered in great stories. It contains the basic patterns that are repeated in all the stages of the storywheel, and when used as a story model, it helps create a bond between the storymaker and the creative unconscious self. See paradigm.

great snake: Another name for the physical archetypes.

great story: A story that becomes powerful and endures or becomes a classic or megahit because it contains the hidden truth.

group phenomena: The fact that organized human groups tend to have the same archetypal structure as the human psyche.

hero: A metaphor of the ego archetype, the hero is, by definition, a person (in real life or story) who makes sacrifices and takes risks for the sake of others.

hero's journey: The hero's progress through the upside of the passage.

hidden truth: The ancient wisdom that has been accumulating in our DNA since the beginning of evolution. The creative unconscious self uses great stories and dreams to communicate this hidden knowledge to the conscious self.

hierarchy: The conscious and unconscious archetypal energies have a pecking order and unequal strengths. The primordial, physical, instinctual self has been superseded by the stronger higher self, and the conscious self is caught in the middle.

high concept: An intriguing story idea that can be stated in a few words and is easy for everyone to relate to and understand. The fewer the words, the higher the concept.

higher consciousness: The quintessential heroic consciousness that can be recovered by retracing the steps of the Golden Paradigm, which is to say our evolutionary path.

higher self: The positive archetypes, governed by the spiritual self, working in concert to accomplish our highest aspirations and goals.

holdfast: The negative, selfish side of the ego.

hook: An intriguing twist given to the story subject being explored.

idealization: An artistic tool of the imagination.

imagination: A largely unconscious, image-making function which helps the storymaker transform psychic energy into useful metaphors.

imitations of real life: An artistic look at how people and other living things really act, communicate, and behave.

inauthentic state: A state of incompleteness or stagnation that has to be resolved before an authentic, heroic state can be achieved. Any state that is less than our full potential.

incident worth repeating: A significant, much talked-about event from which a great story can be evolved.

inciting action: The downside action which causes the problem of the story focus.

initiation: A stage on the **upside** of the **passage** wherein the **ego** and the **hero** perform actions which strengthen consciousness. Compare **regression**.

integration: A stage on the **upside** of the **passage** wherein the **ego** and the **hero** perform actions which bring about the synthesis of discordant aspects of the personality. Compare **alienation**.

Kali Yuga: According to the Hindu religion, the current age of alienation and discord.

legend: A story on the **upside** of the **storywheel** that relates the individual to the world at large.

liberation: The goal of the **higher self**. It seeks to free the **entity** from the tyranny and corruption that caused the **state of misfortune** and create a new, unified whole.

limbic system: The mammalian brain that controls the emotional part of our nature. Compare **neo-cortex** and **R–complex**.

love interest: The positive **anima** and **animus**. They act as go-betweens and are the ego/hero's guide to the soul.

love story: A story whose **dominant plot** has an emotional objective which ends in reunion or separation (tragic love story).

lower self: The negative archetypes, governed by the primordial **physical self**, working in concert.

major players: See **character archetypes**.

make-believe: An act of pretending that creates a safe way of looking objectively at things that occur in real life.

marvelous element: A **metaphor** for the positive powers that enable transformation. Psychologically, they are the building blocks of consciousness. Compare **terrible element**.

meaning: Another word for **wisdom** in a story. See **moral**.

meaningful connection: A realized parallel between the characters and events in a story and our own real-life situations.

mental: The part of our selves that manages thoughts, memories, intelligence, and reason.

mental archetypes: The patterns of energy in our thinking brain (**neo-cortex**) that create knowledge, intelligence, and understanding. In great stories, they are the **wise old man** and **woman** (positive) and the **sorcerer** and **sorceress** (negative).

metaphor: The symbolic language that reveals the **hidden truth**.

miniaturization: An **artistic tool of the imagination**.

modeling: A **creative technique** in which you associate emotionally charged images and ideas with the **archetypes** of the **Golden Paradigm**.

moral: The lessons of a story's action. See **wisdom**.

Mozart effect: A creative stage in which ideas flow effortlessly.

mystery: A story whose **dominant plot** has a mental objective and ends with an enigma or a solution.

myth: A story on the **upside** of the **storywheel** that relates the individual to the spiritual or cosmic self. Compare **anti-myth**.

nadir: The lowest, most negative point on the **storywheel** or **Golden Paradigm**.

narrative structure: The way in which the incidents of a story are arranged for the telling.

nascent ego: The positive, unselfish side of the **ego**. The conscious element on the **upside** of the cycle that is about to be awakened and transformed into **hero** consciousness (a mature ego).

negative: Serving or supporting the interests and objectives of the **lower self**.

neo-cortex: The higher, thinking brain. Compare **limbic system** and **R-complex**.

one and the many: A quality of **metaphor** by which a major **archetype** can be personified by many different **characters** or by one character.

oral tradition: Stories that are passed verbally from generation to generation and not written down.

overreach: Uncontrolled greed. A primary cause of the **antihero's** downfall.

paradigm: A model.

paradise: A **metaphor** for an optimum state of mind.

passage: The cycles of transformation outlined in the **Golden Paradigm**. Known also as the **hero's journey, the path,** or the **whole story.**

the path: The journey of our lives. The cycles of change and growth necessary to reach our full potential. See **passage**.

perseverance: A component of the **universal structure**.

physical: The part of our selves that manages the organs of the body and the needs of the flesh.

physical archetypes: The motivating energies of the **R-complex** (the reptilian brain) and the source of our most basic instincts, appetites, and drives. In great stories, these energies are personified as the positive and negative, male and female, physical parent figures that tempt and corrupt the antihero.

plot: A dramatic action. The virtues that give a story's dominant action its dramatic qualities.

point of view: The vantage point from which a story is told or a problem examined.

positive: Serving the interests of the **higher self**.

possession: The goal of the **lower self**. It seeks to take control of an entity and redirect its goals toward those that fulfill its own desires and needs.

potential: The vast potential is what we could gain if we followed the heroic **passages** revealed by story and outlined in the **Golden Paradigm**.

precedent structures: Underlying motifs found in great stories that can be redressed to create entirely new stories.

principal action: The central, unifying action that solves the problem and brings about a **change of fortune**.

probing the fascination: A **creative technique** that involves working with a **fascination** in ways that bring other story-relevant ideas and images to the surface.

problem solving: A **creative technique** for solving the story problems that emerge when you **test** the **story model**.

protagonist: From the Greek word meaning first actor—hence, the main character in a story.

psyche: The totality of all psychic processes, conscious as well as unconscious. According to Jung, a structure made for movement, growth, change, and transformation. An evolution toward self-realization is embedded in all psychic processes.

R-complex: The reptile brain. It controls the lower, physical, animal side of our nature. Compare **limbic system** and **neo-cortex**.

real life: The real things that are artistically treated to create **metaphors**.

rebirth: A stage on the **upside** of the **passage** wherein the **ego** and the **hero** experience an infusion of higher consciousness which gives them a sense of being reborn. Compare **death**.

reflection: A component of the **universal structure**.

regression: A stage on the **downside** of the **passage** wherein the **holdfast** and the **anti-hero** take actions which weaken consciousness. Compare **initiation**.

relativity: A quality of **metaphor** by which its meaning is determined by its relation to the whole.

resolution: How the actions of a story are resolved. See **classical structure**.

reversal: Achieving the opposite of what was intended in problem solving. See **classical structure**.

rivalry: The archetypes of the **higher** and **lower self** are competing for influence over the conscious self. See **hierarchy**.

romance: A story that exaggerates the nobility and chivalry of its characters and ends happily. Compare **comedy, tragedy, drama**.

sacrifice: A selfless act that defines a **hero**. Without personal sacrifice there is no hero and no **higher consciousness**.

Satan: A **metaphor** of the lower, primordial self.

scene: The most important **unit of action** in a story. It highlights the essential steps, gives them a dramatic structure, and provides a setting that approximates **real life**.

scourge: One of the negative states (injustice, slavery, poverty, disease, death, ignorance, etc.) being created on the **downside** of the **cycle**. Compare **value**.

self: A unifying principle within the human **psyche**. The **creative unconscious**. The sum of all the **archetypes** and our vast **potential**. According to Jung, it is the unity of the personality as a whole. An archetypal urge to coordinate, relativize, and mediate the tension of the opposites. It occupies the central position of authority in relation to psychological life and therefore the destiny of the individual. By way of the self, one is confronted with the polarity of good and evil, human and divine.

separation: A stage on the **upside** of the **passage** wherein the **ego** and the **hero** venture out on their own, seeking a solution to the problem.

shadow: An **archetype** of the **creative unconscious self**. All of the undesirable and inferior aspects of our psychic selves that have been repressed into our personal unconscious. In a story, these repressed elements appear as demons and archvillains.

shapeshifting: The ability of certain **metaphors** to change their shape or cast spells. It reflects the human mind's ability to adjust, change, shift, and be transformed.

solution formula: The right combination of large and small actions used by the hero to solve the story's problem.

sorcerer and sorceress: Negative male and female **mental archetypes**.

spiritual: The higher dimension of our selves that connects us to the mysteries of the universe.

spiritual archetypes: The guiding spirits and hidden wisdom of the higher, unbounded cosmic self. They guard our destiny and inspire us to take positive actions. In great stories, they are the positive and negative, male and female, spiritual parent figures.

state of good fortune: The positive state created within the entity by the **upside** of the **cycle**.

state of misfortune: The state of misery created within the entity by the **downside** of the **cycle**.

story: A term used to signify **great stories** collectively.

story alchemy: The creative stage dominated by **conjuring, testing,** and **problem solving**.

story focus: The aspect of the **whole story** being shown to the audience.

storymaker: The creator of new stories. Compare **storyteller**.

storymaking: The art of creating new stories. Compare **storytelling**.

story model: The **Golden Paradigm**, when it is used as a tool to assist **storymakers**.

storyteller: Someone who relates stories that already exist. Compare **storymaker**.

storytelling: The art of telling a story that already exists. Compare **storymaking**.

storywheel: A model that brings all the different types of **great story** together into one grand design. Viewed in this way, all of the cycles of change and growth we experience from birth to death are revealed, and it becomes apparent that the purpose of great stories is to guide us to higher states of being.

structure: The arrangement of the incidents of a story. **Actions** become structures when they have **meaning**. Structures become **plots** when they produce a dramatic effect.

style: A quality that further defines a person's **character**.

subplot: Subordinate actions necessary to accomplish the objectives of the **dominant plot**.

sugar coat: See **entertainment dimensions**.

technical dimensions: Craft dimensions like variety, contrast, proportion, symmetry, timing, and tempo that help create the **aesthetic dimensions**.

technique: The conscious methods used by artists and **storymakers** to transform psychic energy into visual **metaphors**.

tempter: The negative **animus**. He is the corrupter of the feminine **antihero**. Psychologically, he is a critical inner voice.

temptress: The negative **anima**; the femme fatale; the male **antihero**'s guide to the underworld.

terrible element: A metaphor for the destructive, negative powers coveted by the **lower self**. Compare **marvelous element**.

testing: A creative technique that helps a **storymaker** try out the **story model**.

theme: The subject being explored in the **story focus**.

threshold guardian: An **archetype** of the **creative unconscious self**. Threshold guardians stand in the way of the conscious archetypes and are there to test their readiness and resolve.

tragedy: A story that exaggerates the nobility of its characters and ends unhappily. Compare **comedy, romance, drama.**

transcendental story: A story whose dominant plot has a spiritual aspect.

trial and error: An important component of the **universal structure.**

trickster: An **archetype** of the **creative unconscious self.** Tricksters are troublemakers who goad the conscious archetypes forward when they are stuck.

unconscious self: That part of the **psyche** that operates without our **conscious** awareness. In story, it is an unfamiliar, dark, or supernatural world and its denizens.

units of action: The building blocks of action—i.e., the beats, shots, scenes, sequences, and acts that make up a film or play, and the sentences, paragraphs, chapters, and books of a novel.

unity: The thematic elements that make a story one.

universal structure: One of the four structures of a problem-solving **principal action.** Its key elements are trial and error, reflection, and perseverance.

upside: The positive first half of the **passage.** Compare **downside.**

value: One of the positive goals (justice, freedom, wisdom, life, health, etc.) being pursued on the **upside** of the **passage.** Compare **scourge.**

vast potential: See **potential.**

vilification: An **artistic tool of the imagination.**

war story: A story whose **dominant plot** has a physical objective which ends in victory or defeat.

whole story: The larger background or frame story that covers one complete cycle or **passage** of the **Golden Paradigm** and creates the context for the **story focus.**

wisdom: The special knowledge revealed by a story's action. The **hidden truth** concealed by a story's **sugar coat.** See **meaning, moral.**

wise old man and wise old woman: Positive male and female **mental archetypes.**

yin and yang: The Chinese symbol of opposites.

zenith: The highest, most positive point on the **storywheel** or **Golden Paradigm.**

Index

Individuation, 23, 83
Initiation, 69, 70, 71
Inspiration, 16
Integration, 69, 70
Iphigenia, 130
Ironic comedy, 6

J
Jack and the Beanstalk, 15,16, 22, 44, 86
Jaws, 44, 57, 76, 112, 120, 137, 142, 144, 180, 187, 197
Jesus, 22, 157, 191
JFK, 168
Judgment at Nuremberg, 134
Julius Caesar, 19
Jung, C. G., xi, 12, 23, 27, 61, 66, 71, 83
Jungle Book, 80
Jurassic Park, 56, 76, 120, 148, 157

K
Kali Yuga, 10
King Arthur, 21, 22, 80, 135-136, 137, 157, 191
King David, 69, 70, 125, 126, 157
King Herod, 69
King Lear, 157
King, Martin Luther, 67, 105
King Solomon's Mines, 122
Knowledge, 164
Kramer vs Kramer, 68

L
Lancelot, 91
La Pensera, 175
The Last of the Mohicans, 119
Lawson, John Howard, 7
Legends, 23, 155
Lethal Weapon, 122
Liberation, 98
Libido, 12, 75
The Lifeguard, 152
Limbic system, 63, 78
The Lion King, 47, 81, 82, 157, 179, 181, 182, 186
Little Caesar, 69, 126, 157
The Longest Day, 88, 137
Lorenzo's Oil, 182
Lost Horizons, 27, 157
Lost potential, 21
Love interest, 59, 83, 88, 105
Love story, 142
Lower self, 60, 71, 72, 75, 76, 79, 80, 96, 146

THE WRITER'S JOURNEY
MYTHIC STRUCTURE FOR WRITERS - 2ND EDITION
Christopher Vogler

This new edition provides fresh insights and observations from Vogler's ongoing work with mythology's influence on stories, movies, and humankind itself.

Learn why thousands of professional writers have made THE WRITER'S JOURNEY a best-seller and why it is considered required reading by many of Hollywood's top studios! Learn how master storytellers have used mythic structure to create powerful stories that tap into the mythological core which exists in us all.

Writers of both fiction and non-fiction will discover a set of useful myth-inspired storytelling paradigms (e.g., The Hero's Journey) and step-by-step guidelines to plot and character development. Based on the work of Joseph Campbell, THE WRITER'S JOURNEY is a must for writers of all kinds.

New analyses of box office blockbusters such as Titanic, The Lion King, The Full Monty, Pulp Fiction, and Star Wars.

• A foreword describing the worldwide reaction to the first edition and the continued influence of The Hero's Journey model.

• Vogler's new observations on the adaptability of THE WRITER'S JOURNEY for international markets, and the changing profile of the audience.

• The latest observations and techniques for using the mythic model to enhance modern storytelling.

• New subject index and filmography.

• How to apply THE WRITER'S JOURNEY paradigm to your own life.

Book-of-the-Month Club Selection • Writer's Digest Book Club Selection
Movie Entertainment Book Club Selection

$22.95, 300 pages, 6 x 9
ISBN 0-941188-70-1
Order # 2598RLS

MICHAEL WIESE PRODUCTIONS
11288 Ventura Blvd., Suite 821
Studio City, CA 91604
1-818-379-8799
kenlee@earthlink.net
www.mwp.com

Write or Fax
for a
free catalog.

Please send me the following
books:

Title	Order Number (#RLS___)	Amount
_____	_____
_____	_____
_____	_____
_____	_____

SHIPPING _____

California Tax (8.25%) _____

TOTAL ENCLOSED _____

Please make check or money order payable to
Michael Wiese Productions

(Check one) ___ Master Card ___Visa ____Amex

Credit Card Number_____

Expiration Date_____

Cardholder's Name_____

Cardholder's Signature_____

SHIP TO:

Name_____

Address_____

City_____ State_____ Zip_____